IT'S ALL PRICKS AND BALLS THIS CHRISTMAS

&

GIBLET STEW

RITA JOHN

First published in Great Britain in 2024

Copyright © Rita John

The moral right of this author has been asserted.

All rights reserved.

No part of this publication may be reproduced, stored in a retrieval system, or transmitted, in any form or by any means, without the prior permission in writing of the publisher, nor be otherwise circulated in any form of binding or cover other than that in which it is published and without a similar condition including this condition being imposed on the subsequent purchaser.

Editing, design, typesetting and publishing by UK Book Publishing

www.ukbookpublishing.com

ISBN: 978-1-917329-44-6

IT'S ALL PRICKS AND BALLS THIS CHRISTMAS & GIBLET STEW

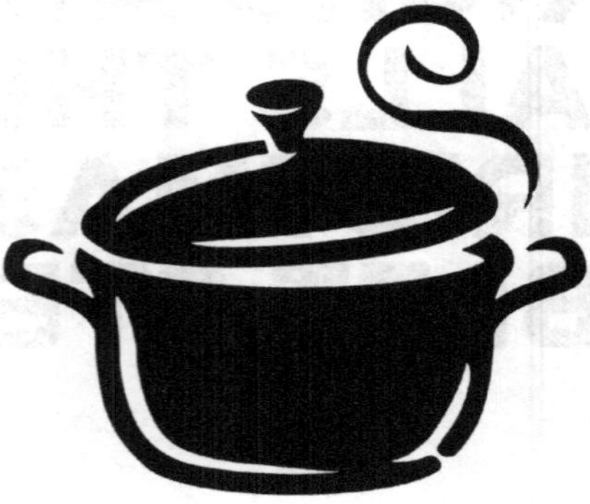

CHAPTER 1

I was a twenty-two-year-old married woman the day I walked into my part-time job at the pub. It was part of a well-known chain of pubs and restaurants in the mid-1970s: Trophy Taverns. My full-time job was as a manageress for a national home decorating company, Crown Wallpapers, which had three shops in our city centre.

It was around the time when big chains like B&Q were starting up. These big chains ultimately led to the closure of our Crown Wallpaper stores. My store had just closed, and the empty premises had been taken over by Holland and Barrett, which still occupies that shop to this day.

I was moved to one of our two remaining shops as manageress, where I remained for about a year. It was during this time that I took the part-time job at the pub – not only to help with finances at home but also because the man I had married (who was about thirteen years older than me and who had seemed worldly with a job as a machinist at a well-established factory in the city when we wed) turned out to be a womaniser, drinker, and gambler.

My childhood had been truly horrible, marked by physical and emotional abuse at the hands of my mother. I was the eldest of four children. After me came my brother Ronald, two years younger (my mother's "star child" who could do no wrong), followed by my sister Vicki a year later, and then Rita, the youngest. Rita had been born disabled. In those days, before political correctness became widespread, she was referred to as a "spastic" or "backwards". She didn't walk a step until she was three years old. I was tasked with her care, taking her everywhere with me and generally looking after her, which didn't bother me – she was, after all, my sister, and I loved her. What did upset me, however, was that no matter what I did for her or for my mother, I remained the target of my mother's anger.

When I was seven years old, after a particularly bad beating, I decided to leave home. My plan was to go to London to find work. I had collected a few bits and pieces – soap, towels, etc. – and packed them in a school satchel. One afternoon, I left home and made my way to the local pit head at Keresley

Colliery, where Dad worked. I knew there was a barn along the way where I intended to sleep.

However, on my way, I ran into a group of boys who were out playing. They asked me what I was doing out so late. I explained my plan, mentioning the barn, but they told me it was full of rats. That ruined my sleeping arrangement and threw my plan into chaos. When I arrived at the pit head, I hung around outside the colliery office for a bit. A miner on his way to see the pit nurse asked me what I was doing out so late, as it was now getting dark. I told him I was waiting for my dad and quickly walked away, realising people were starting to question why I was out at such a young age.

I then started walking back down the railway line toward the main road. As I made my way along the tracks, headlights appeared behind me, which was odd because no trains ran on that line overnight. I ducked to the side to let the vehicle pass, but it pulled up behind me. A nurse got out and, walking towards me, called my name. The miner who had spoken to me earlier had told the pit nurse about me, and she knew something wasn't right – a young child being out so late. She had organised a search party. She held me close as we walked down the railway line to the main road, where a group of our neighbours, including my dad, were searching for me. Dad was thrilled to see me, and I was relieved to see him. However, I was terrified of seeing my mother.

When we got home, my dad defended me to my mum. Instead of the beating I had expected, I was allowed to go straight to bed, although I was still locked into the bedroom I shared with my two sisters.

Our house was a miner's home on Houldsworth Crescent, Exhall. A miner's wage included his house. Dad worked at the local coal mine until he had an accident. The coal face collapsed on him during a shift, effectively pushing his head into his back and crushing some vertebrae in his spine. Luckily, he had his miner's helmet on, which saved him from death.

His injuries resulted in him staying at our local hospital, the Coventry and Warwickshire, for over a year. He spent that time on his back in what they called "traction" in those days. During his hospitalisation, I had an accident at school and broke my arm. After having my arm put in a cast at the same hospital's A&E where Dad was, Mum took me up to the ward where he was staying. Back then, about 65 years ago, children were not allowed to visit adults in hospitals, as the rules were very strict. Mum took my coat off so my cast was visible and told me that the Sister might let me see my dad for a few minutes – and she did.

I was shocked when I saw him. I had to stand on a step beside his bed so I could see him, and he could see me, as he was completely immobile in a contraption of pulleys and weights. His head was suspended in a metal cage with weights hanging from it, over the end of the hospital bed. Mum explained that these weights were very slowly pulling Dad's head back out of his shoulders to relieve the pressure on the compacted vertebrae caused by the coal face collapsing on him. It had to be done slowly, or it would have killed him. No wonder children weren't allowed to visit – it was extremely traumatic to see.

Before Dad's accident, during the summer months, he would load us three able-bodied kids into a cart he had made and take us up to the railway line that ran from the pit head across the farmer's fields at the end of our road. All of that has gone now, replaced by an industrial estate and houses. The train track is still there, but it's used to transport cargo from the industrial estate built on what was once the farmer's fields to various cities.

We would scavenge coal nuggets that had fallen from the overloaded coal trains as they passed down the line. These scavenged nuggets were added to our winter coal supply. Every miner's house had an outdoor loo and coal shed, and as part of a miner's wages, each family received a ton of coal a month.

This was invaluable in winter when other families would freeze because coal was not cheap, but while Dad worked at the pit, we stayed fairly warm in winter.

On one of these scavenger trips, I found a massive lump of coal and gleefully ran toward Dad, completely unaware of a coiled adder directly in front of me. My brother saw what was about to happen and rushed toward me, kicking my foot out from under me and causing me to crash to the ground. He saved me from being bitten, which could have been really serious. I can honestly say that was the one and only time my brother ever did anything nice for me in my life.

To my horror, Dad then sent me home to get a container to catch the snake and keep it for my brother! Watching Dad trying to capture that loathsome reptile was terrifying, but my brother insisted on having it, so it was caught. To my immense relief, when we got home, Mum wasn't having any of it, so the snake was released back into the field behind our house, which ran between the pit and our home. I was surprised, as my brother usually got whatever he wanted. But thank God he didn't get that.

One drawback of our coal allowance, however, was that in winter, when every family in the city burned coal, it caused thick smog – a combination of fog and coal smoke. These smogs could last for days, and you couldn't see a hand in front of your face. They also deadened noise, creating a very eerie atmosphere. Our parents didn't like us going out in the smog, as it affected our breathing quite badly.

I can still remember the gas lamp man coming down our street to light the gas street lamps every night. Our area, Exhall, was one of the last streets to get modern streetlights, as we were semi-rural at that time.

I also remember the milkman delivering milk from large churns on the back of his horse-drawn dray. He would dip a metal jug into the milk and pour it into whatever containers the housewives provided. My granddad would see the milkman coming up the street and call me over. He'd give me some sugar to feed to the horse while he stood at the back end, waiting for the horse muck to appear, which it always did while the horse was eating. Granddad would then take the "liquid gold" around to the back of the house to spread on his rhubarb and other vegetables, as did most households back then. Nothing went to waste – not even horse muck.

Behind our house, a field separated the houses from the pit, and a stream ran through it. The source of the stream came from the pit, which was always on fire. This made the stream warm, and at one point, a pool of water collected. Us kids loved going to this pool because the water was warm, and we could catch newts, which we thought were baby dragons (though they're endangered now). However, we were eventually stopped from going there after one of our friends put her hands in the pond to catch a newt, not realising the pond edge had started to burn again. She suffered severe burns – long before the days of health and safety.

Every Saturday, we kids would head to the last bend in the train track from the pit head, where there was a high embankment. We'd sit and wait for the last train, as no matter how often it happened, it was always the same. The train, overloaded with trucks, would struggle to manage the tight turn, and like clockwork, it would derail. The pit would then send a crane to lift the engine and trucks back onto the track. It was a great source of amusement for us kids. By the time the officials had managed to manoeuvre the massive crane down the tight railway line, we'd already scavenged as much loose coal as we could. The officials tried to shoo us away, but we saw no danger – just fun and free coal.

By the time the coal trucks were back on the tracks, they were much lighter, as we'd stashed the coal in hiding spots, ready to take to our parents' coal sheds once the officials left. We literally ran rings around them. The scavenged coal helped supplement our winter coal allowance. Eventually, someone at the pit head caught on and started sending two trains down on Saturdays, preventing the derailments. This not only spoiled our fun but also saved the pit money on hiring cranes and losing coal.

The smogs we suffered every winter were one of the reasons for the rise of gas central heating in the years to come. It took about fifteen years before our family had a house with central heating. Until then, families heated water with a coal fire in the lounge, which had a boiler behind it in the upstairs bedroom. Some houses, like my gran's, had a copper in the kitchen, which was lit once a week on wash day to heat water. Otherwise, you boiled a kettle. The copper was usually in a corner of the kitchen, and you lit a fire underneath it through a small opening at floor level to heat the water in the large bowl-shaped vessel. If they still existed today, they'd be worth a fortune.

Even in winter, we only lit the fireplace in the lounge. The bedrooms were freezing, as you didn't light fires in the bedroom fireplaces – not only because of the danger to children with open fires but also because it would deplete your coal supply, which had to last all winter. Still, we were luckier than most families who couldn't afford coal and literally froze all winter, sometimes finding ice in their beds. We only had frost flowers on the inside of our bedroom windows, not in our actual beds. We escaped the ice in our beds thanks to the residual heat from the lounge coal fire warming the boiler behind our bedroom fireplace. But let me tell you, you didn't hang about getting dressed in the morning!

CHAPTER 2

After Dad came home from the hospital, he had to wear a metal collar to support his head. He wore it for a year before switching to a foam collar. In those days, there was no such thing as compensation for miners after a workplace accident. Plus, a miner's home was tied to his job, so when Dad was deemed unable to return to work, the pit evicted us from our house. No job, no house. We were lucky in a way – the mine had allowed us to stay in the house for quite some time after Dad's accident. But once the collar came off, it was goodbye collar, goodbye job, goodbye house. The house was needed for Dad's replacement at the mine.

My mother's brother, Uncle Raymond, and his wife, Aunt Elizabeth, lived in the centre of town on Read Street in Hillfields. They told my parents that the house at the opposite end of their terrace had become vacant.

So, we moved into this two-up, two-down derelict house. When I say derelict, I don't exaggerate. These houses had stood empty for some years and were in appalling condition. The one we moved into had actually been damaged in a fire, and the whole row was condemned by the council. These houses were over a hundred years old. As I'm sure you're aware, councils move very slowly when it comes to demolishing slums, so while they dithered, homeless families like ours moved in and made do. Today, we would have been called squatters.

As you entered the front door, you stepped into a room, then passed an under-the-stairs cupboard into the main lounge, and down a step into the kitchen. The toilet was outside, but Dad knocked a door through the end wall of the kitchen so us kids wouldn't have to go outside at night to use the toilet.

The kitchen itself was unstable. Dad had shored up the walls with timber, pinning plywood across the frame to resemble some sort of walls. The water pipes were made of lead, so every time we wanted water, we had to run the tap for ten minutes to flush out any lead that had settled to avoid lead poisoning.

The stairs to the bedrooms were accessed through a door in the back left-hand corner of the middle room, situated between the front room and the kitchen. We couldn't walk up the middle of the stairs because the fire that had damaged the house had burned through the centre of them. If you stepped on the middle, you'd drop straight through into the under-the-stairs cupboard.

Speaking of that cupboard, it was the setting for a funny event. Back then, cereal manufacturers would include all sorts of toys in their products to encourage children to bug their parents into buying whatever cereal had the best prize. One cereal came with a ghost-shaped toy that was supposed to glow in the dark. My mother fished it out of the box and said, "When your brother comes home, tell him to fetch a dirty tea towel from the cupboard under the stairs. I'll hide under there behind the coats, and when he reaches for the cloth, I'll float the ghost out and scare him."

I did as she asked. From my vantage point in the kitchen, I watched as my brother looked for the cloth. My mother had positioned herself in the cupboard, and there was a small sofa at a right angle in front of it. Suddenly, my brother leapt from his kneeling position over the back of the sofa in one gigantic leap. I was in awe – he landed, blubbering and shouting, "There's an arm coming out of the wall under the stairs!"

He hadn't even seen the supposedly glowing ghost in my mother's hand – all he saw was a disembodied arm emerging from the wall. My mother burst out laughing as she crawled out from under the stairs, clutching the small ghost. My brother was so freaked out, but laughter is infectious. I started laughing, not only at my brother's face, which was contorted in shock, but also at my mother's uncontrollable laughter and the way my brother had cleared that sofa in one bound.

To be honest, laughter like that was a rarity in our house.

We had a Jack Russell terrier named Rocky. Every time someone went to the loo, Rocky, who we bought from a local pet shop (back when they were still allowed to sell dogs and cats), would stand by the door and dart in before you sat down. His job was to catch any rats that might be passing by. When we first got Rocky, he was so weak he could barely stand, rocking back and forth on his unsteady legs – hence the name. In hindsight, he must have been too young to leave his mother, but we soon got him fit.

Rocky was always on guard, and we never went to the toilet without him. It just wasn't safe! The rats could sense Rocky, and with him around, they wouldn't appear, so you could do your business in peace.

One day, as I opened the toilet door, Rocky shot inside and caught a rat that had been scurrying by. The rat screamed, I screamed, and I bolted, running past my startled dad, who was working in the kitchen. I flew past my mum in the lounge, shouting, "Rocky has a rat!" Mum rushed after me, and we both ended up standing on chairs in the front room as Rocky ran after us, proudly holding the dead rat in his mouth, with a look that said, "Look what I've done!" Dad, now over his initial shock, came to get the rat from Rocky, praising him for protecting the family. Rocky got an extra bone that day as a reward.

Rocky was bought to replace my first dog, Prince. I had Prince from a puppy, and he moved with us to the derelict house from our coal miner's home. When Prince was young, he got into a fight with a much larger dog that bit him on his back. After that, every now and then, his back legs would give out, and he'd have fits.

Prince usually came with us on holidays, but one morning, just before we were leaving, he was gone. I asked Mum where he was, and she said he'd had a bad fit, so Dad took him to the vet. When Dad came back without him, he said the vet was going to board Prince in the kennels until we returned. I thought nothing of it, as Mum had put him in kennels before when we went away.

When we returned from holiday, Mum sent Dad to get Prince from the vet, but Dad came back alone. He told me that Prince had taken a turn for the worse and died while we were away, and the vet couldn't save him. I was devastated and heartbroken.

Years later, though, Dad told me the truth. My mother had actually sent Prince to the vet to be put down the day we left for holiday. He'd had a fit, but she simply didn't want to deal with him anymore. When I found out, I was furious and heartbroken all over again. I really hated my mother for that – she was cold-hearted and callous.

Every Sunday, Dad would pull the roasting tin out of the oven, which still had last week's meat fat in it. We only had meat once a week, usually something cheap like ox heart, which Mum would boil and then slice in gravy. It was tasty and only cost threepence since it was considered offal – something typically fed to dogs; but for us poor families, it was a good source of iron. In the tin, you could always see the footprints of the mice and rats that had wandered through the leftover fat during the week. Mum used to say they were living in the back of our cooker. Dad would scrub the tin before cooking any kind of Sunday meal in it again.

We didn't have a bathroom. Every Sunday night, Dad would boil water in metal buckets on the cooker and pour it into a tin bath in the kitchen. Mum would take her bath first, followed by my dad, and then us kids would take turns using the same water. My sisters and I were usually shoved into the bath together to save water.

The house was haunted, too. One Mother's Day, I got up early to make Mum breakfast in bed. I crept downstairs with a tray, planning to put her breakfast on it. As I pushed open the door to the lounge, I looked across the room at the sash window. By the window, Mum had a clothes horse with some laundry drying on it. Half-asleep, I noticed a cone-shaped figure standing by the clothes horse, almost like a Klu Klux Klan shape. At first, I thought it was just oddly shaped laundry hanging there. But then it turned to look at me, and I saw glowing yellow slits for eyes. I realised I was looking at something supernatural.

I ran back upstairs and dived into my bottom bunk, shaking the bed so much that it woke my sister, who was sleeping in the top bunk. She yelled at me, asking what I was doing, and I told her there was a ghost downstairs. She came down the ladder, shouting at me that I was being stupid. But as she headed for the door to the stairs, it suddenly flung open, and she shot back into the room, screaming, "It's coming up the stairs!"

By this time, Dad was up, and we were both babbling incoherently. When he calmed us down and asked what was going on, my sister described the ghost as all white, with a pointed head and glowing yellow eyes – exactly what I had seen.

I hadn't given my sister any description of the ghost, only that there was one. Even now, more than 60 years later, the hairs on the back of my neck still stand on end when I think about it. Thankfully, that was the only time I saw the apparition.

Don't let anyone tell you that ghosts don't exist. I know for sure that they do.

CHAPTER 3

Our school was just up the road from where we lived, and we kids had a little chant we used to sing about it:

Come to Southfields, come to Southfields,
Live a life of misery.
There is a signpost saying welcome, welcome unto thee.
Build a bonfire, build a bonfire,
Put the teachers on the top.
Put old Webby in the middle,
And burn the bloody lot!

"Webby" was our headmistress, Mrs Webster – a nasty piece of work.

Mrs Webster once had my father arrested, despite him being the most honest man I've ever known.

Someone had broken into her office and stolen her purse, which was left in her handbag. This was back when schools were open, and anyone could walk in at any time, unlike the lockdowns we have today. The police showed up at our house and took Dad to the central station, removing his shoelaces and belt as though he might harm himself.

It terrified him. It brought back memories of Belsen and the Gestapo during the war. My mother rushed to get a solicitor, and when he spoke with the police, they explained that Mrs Webster had accused my father because he wore a donkey jacket, like the one seen near her office at the time of the theft. That was her only reason for accusing him – his coat. But Dad had been at work when the theft occurred, and his boss confirmed exactly where he was at the time.

The police released Dad without charges, but the damage was done. The ordeal reawakened all his memories of Belsen, and his nightmares returned. In those days, there was no redress for defamation or even an apology from Mrs Webster. Dad never went near that school again, and it seemed our little chant wasn't far from the truth.

The experience stirred up the trauma of Dad's time in Belsen. He never really talked much about it, but sometimes the nightmares were so intense, he would wake up screaming. He shared a few things with me – things I'll never forget.

Each morning in Belsen, the Gestapo would line up the prisoners and force the person at the end of the line to pick a number. Whatever number they chose, the Gestapo would shoot the prisoner who fell under that number, in the head, then start again from the chosen number, killing the next person, and so on. It was a cruel way of making the prisoners feel responsible for their own friends' deaths.

There was also the cesspit, which served the camp and was pumped out at intervals. One winter, Dad's best friend went missing during the morning roll call. Days later, when they emptied the cesspit, his friend's frozen body was found stuck to the side. The rats had eaten away his fingers. He had probably hidden there to escape the shootings but either froze to death or was overcome by the fumes.

Dad never ate turnips after Belsen. Turnips were the only food he could scavenge to survive. At night, dodging searchlights and patrols, he'd sneak to the Gestapo food dump to grab turnips, which were often covered in mould. He'd just wipe off the mould and eat them – it was that or starve. By the time the camp was liberated, Dad weighed only four stone (56 pounds).

Mrs Webster's accusation dragged all of those memories back to the surface for him. She had no idea the damage she'd caused, and there was no justice for Dad. But her actions left a scar that I'll never forgive.

My sister Rita, apart from being disabled, also wouldn't eat meat. She suffered from fits and took phenobarbitals to control them. One lunchtime at Southfields School, her teacher, Mrs Butler – a woman who wore tons of makeup and was always dressed in the height of fashion, and who you could smell before you saw her, thanks to the cloud of perfume that preceded her – decided she was going to force Rita to eat the meat on her plate. When Rita refused, Mrs Butler shook her so hard and for so long that it sent her into a fit.

Once again, my mother went to the police, accompanied by my father, to lodge a complaint. The police sergeant who dealt with them said something I've never forgotten: "Sorry, these teachers are too well-protected in these schools. My advice to you is to catch that teacher on her own, where no one can see, and give her a beating."

My father, of course, would never do such a thing. He wouldn't lay a hand on any woman, even my mother – despite her often physically assaulting him in front of us. If anyone deserved a beating, it was my mother. So, my parents went to Mrs Webster, the headmistress, but once again, she didn't want to know, and not even an apology was given.

Across from the school entrance was a row of historic Cash's weavers' houses. Cash's was a world-renowned weaving firm that even made emblems and uniforms for the Royal Family. These houses were built so that the weavers could live and work in the same place, cutting down on absenteeism. Built in the late 18th and early 19th centuries, these houses were considered innovative for their time. The top floors contained looms powered by steam engines, with one engine at each end of a row of three houses. These engines powered the looms across all three rows, which were interconnected through the top floor, allowing any neighbour to access another's home through the shared loft space.

By the late 1950s and early 1960s, these houses, like ours, had been condemned and were awaiting demolition. They were rat-infested, many still had gas lighting, and they were heated by a single coal fire in the living room. We'd wake up on winter mornings with ice on the inside of our bedroom windows. Most families, including ours, couldn't afford enough blankets to keep warm, so we used any coats we had as bed covers. But even then, we often froze at night. If you were lucky, you shared a bed with a sibling for body heat. Sometimes Mum would put a pop bottle filled with hot water, wrapped in a rag, at the bottom of the bed to keep us warm. The rag was to prevent our feet from burning.

In those days, everything was recyclable. We'd scavenge the streets for discarded glass bottles, which we could return to the off licence for pennies or use them as bed warmers in the winter. No duvets back then! My bed, which I shared with Rita, had a couple of my dad's old army blankets, given to him when he was discharged. We also had string bags for groceries – those things could hold a massive amount of shopping, and like everything else, they were reusable. So don't let any young whippersnapper tell me that our generation is responsible for destroying the Earth.

Across from the school, on South Street, there was another row of terraced houses – these ones home to the local prostitutes. We kids would play a game of "spot the punter", watching as the women brought men back and forth from their houses to the local pub, The Brewer and Baker, at the end of the terrace.

Today, that pub is still standing, though it's been turned into student accommodation since our city became a major university hub. The Brewer and Baker is a listed building, and while all the surrounding houses have been demolished, it remains, along with the old school, which is also a listed building, and the factory where my dad worked as a labourer for a time. That factory has since been turned into a storage facility where people can rent spaces for their belongings.

At the other end of our street was the Catholic Church, which provided us kids with some amusement every Sunday. We'd wait outside to see who could spot the priest as he left the church and headed to the Weaver's Arms, the pub at the bottom of the road. It's still there today, though now it's a restaurant called the Hadramud, catering to students. Every Sunday, we'd watch the priest stagger out of the Weaver's Arms, drunk, barely able to stand, and we'd roll around laughing as he struggled to make his way back to the church for the next mass.

Across from the church was a butcher's shop, located on the corner of Hood Street and Raglan Street. But it wasn't just any butcher's – it was a front for the local hard man. He spent more time in jail than at the shop, which was a real sorrow for the locals. To the police, he was a menace, like our version of the Krays, but to the local mothers, he was Robin Hood. While his shop was open, he sold meat cheaply to the locals, his way of caring for the community. In return, the mothers would give him a heads-up if they caught wind of any police activity, ensuring a continued supply of cheap meat for their families.

IT'S ALL PRICKS AND BALLS THIS CHRISTMAS, & GIBLET STEW

Times were tough for us. My dad worked as a labourer at the factory next to our house, but he was still recovering from a spinal injury, and his wages were paltry. Mum, fortunately, got a job in the factory's canteen, which was a godsend. Without that job, we would've starved. Any leftover food from the canteen found its way into our tummies, but even then, many days we missed at least one meal. If it weren't for free school dinners and the canteen, we wouldn't have managed at all.

Every now and then, if Dad could scrape together a few extra pennies, he'd send me to the game shop on Far Gosford Street late on a Saturday afternoon. The shop sold rabbits, chickens, and pigeons – most of which were killed in dubious ways – but to us poor locals, it was a lifeline. Back then, there were no sell-by dates. Unless the food was so rank it could walk off the shelf on its own, we didn't turn our noses up at cheap food. If you timed it right on a Saturday, you could get three pounds of chicken giblets for threepence. If you were lucky, those giblets would consist mostly of gizzards, livers, and hearts with a few necks thrown in. If you got there late, it was mostly chicken necks, but Dad could make a stew out of those giblets that would last the family nearly a week.

There was no refrigeration in those days, so autumn, winter, and spring weren't so bad, as food didn't spoil as quickly. But there was no giblet stew in summer – it just wouldn't keep. Back then, you could only get certain meats in certain months, and pork was only eaten in months with an "R" in them.

Dad made the best giblet stew ever. These days, if there were food shortages, most people would starve – but not me or my family. When you've had to survive on the type of ingredients we had back then, you learn not to be picky. There was nothing better than hot, steaming giblet stew with a big fat dumpling on top in the dead of winter. Or a thick slice of cow's udder with brown sauce, or ox cheek, which you told the butcher was for your dog but was really for your dinner. Nowadays, ox cheek is considered gourmet thanks to celebrity chefs, but back then, it was cheap. And the best of all was ox tongue – pure meat and only threepence. A whole ox heart was also a bargain, though you had to boil it forever to tenderise it. But once cooked, it was delicious, and the water it was boiled in made the most amazing gravy. We didn't waste anything back then – there wasn't enough to waste.

We also ate chitterlings – compressed pigs' intestines that smelled like they'd been dragged through the muck but were still edible. Cow heel, pigs' trotters, and tripe cooked in milk and onions with a few potatoes thrown in were other staples. On Saturdays, my Gran and I would walk into Coventry Market just before closing. Since there were no refrigerators, the stallholders would sell off their perishable stock for pennies. We'd come back well-stocked with fruit and vegetables, and if we got salad, it was a real bonus.

Despite the derelict houses, vermin, and lack of food, I look back on my childhood with mixed feelings. It was poor, dirty, dark, and abusive – but to this day, when I'm feeling down, I make a type of chicken giblet stew to cheer myself up. It brings back memories of my dad and my childhood, and nothing tastes better when you need a little comfort.

Our neighbour, the manageress of the canteen where Mum worked, was also named Violet like my mum. She lived next door to us with her partner, an Irishman. I don't think they were married – they just lived together. He was a real drunk. Every night, he'd come home roaring drunk and beat poor Violet. Us kids would lie in bed listening to her screams. One particularly bad night, we heard him slamming things around and shouting that the dinner she'd given him wasn't enough for a working man. He yelled, "What do you call this? A spoon of peas and a slice of meat? That's not a dinner!" Mum figured Violet must have brought him a canteen dinner from work.

The fight between Violet and the Irishman escalated quickly, the usual screams giving way to blood-curdling cries that pierced the night. Concerned for her safety, Dad went out our back door to see if he could help. Just as he did, Violet burst out of her own back door, frantically fleeing from Irish, who was trying to stab her with a carving knife. Dad tackled him, knocking him out cold. Violet had been stabbed, but fortunately, only in the arm.

Dad wanted to call the police, but Violet refused, insisting we just leave him there. In those days, domestic violence was a grim reality, especially in poorer communities. It was common to see a woman with a black eye; when asked by a neighbour what happened, the usual response was, "I was chopping sticks for the fire and a piece flew up into my eye." Everyone knew what that really meant.

The stresses of poverty often resulted in men taking their frustrations out on their wives. Unlike today, when domestic violence is more acknowledged and police are trained to handle it, back then it was a harsh norm. So, Dad left Irish where he lay, as Violet insisted, she didn't want him back in her house. Mum bandaged Violet's arm, and we all turned in for the night as snow began to fall on the prone body of Irish. When we woke the next morning, he was gone, and we never saw him again.

After that night, Violet ensured that Mum never returned home from work empty-handed. As a result, we had fewer days of hunger than before, thanks to Dad saving her life.

Eventually, the council started relocating families from those hovels. At least we no longer had to deal with dirt and vermin. The council house we moved into had a bathroom, but the conditions were cramped. The only way to heat water was with a coal fire situated in the kitchen, which heated a water tank located above the chimney breast in the back bedroom.

Mum and Dad had a bedroom to themselves, while my brother, Mum's star child, had his own room. The three of us girls had to share a room, which was so small that we needed bunk beds and a single bed. The space between them was so narrow that you couldn't walk between the bunk beds and the single bed. If you needed anything from the airing cupboard in our room, you had to shove the beds together to open the door just enough – about six inches – so you could wriggle out the things you needed.

CHAPTER 4

By now, I had just left school and had been offered an apprenticeship with a local hairdresser. I had a knack for hair, but Mum wouldn't hear of it; the wage was only two pounds a week. Short-sighted, she insisted I go to Woolworths instead, where I could earn five pounds a week selling biscuits.

I was desperate to join the police force, but back then, you had to be eighteen to enlist, so I had three more years to wait. To be fair, the job at Woolworths wasn't bad. I worked on the biscuit and cake counter, where biscuits were sold loose by the pound, with only a few packaged options available.

On Saturday mornings, the biscuit counter had queues stretching all around it. My favourite biscuits were maple walnut creams, but our family couldn't afford to buy biscuits by the pound. However, any broken biscuits were sold off cheap. Since I worked the counter, I usually managed to sneak a couple of unbroken maple walnut creams into the bag of broken biscuits I bought for my family every Saturday.

Even though I was working full-time at age fifteen, I was still my mother's slave. I had to take care of all the household cooking, cleaning, and chores while my three siblings enjoyed their carefree lives. I would come home from work on Thursday afternoons – half days at Woolworths – only to be confronted with a week's worth of washing for a household of six.

When we lived in the derelict house on Read Street, Hillfields, Mum used to rely on the bag wash man to handle the family's laundry. This man would collect our washing, which we stuffed into a pillowcase with our name on it. He drove around in a van to pick up the bags, then took them to his wash place on Vecqueray Street, where he employed a number of Asian women. As you passed by his establishment, you could smell the soap and hear the lively sound of Asian music while these ladies washed everyone's clothes by hand.

At Read Street, we didn't have much laundry to do, as we didn't own many clothes, towels, or sheets due to my parents' poor wages. Towels and sheets were considered luxury items. But when the council moved us to the house on Elkington Street, Courthouse Green, both my parents found slightly better jobs. Dad became a driver for the British Oxygen Company based in Terry Road, while Mum held various jobs before landing a pest control officer position with Coventry City Council. With their improved earnings, we could finally afford essentials like sheets and blankets for six beds instead of using our coats as blankets, as we had previously. Consequently, my Thursday wash now included all the bedding along with every other household item.

I would stand by the sink with a rubbing board – a rectangular piece of wood fitted with ribbed glass – where I rubbed hard soap and worked the dirty clothes across it to remove stains. I also used a posher, a round piece of metal with holes in it, attached to a wooden pole, which was like an upturned pudding bowl. The holes allowed for a beating action as I pounded the clothes in a bowl of soapy water. This was really hard graft. There were no washing machines in those days; everything had to be hand-washed, just a step up from beating clothes against a stone in a stream.

I did all of this without food or drink. You were lucky if you got a cup of tea in the morning before heading out to work. Mum always made sure she had her cigarettes; she smoked Woodbines while Dad preferred Capstan full strength.

On Fridays, Woolworths closed at 7:30, so by the time I got home, it would be almost 8:15. The ironing from the previous day's wash would be waiting for me. With no electric irons available, we used old heat-on-the-fire irons. They had to be just the right temperature – not too hot, or they would scorch the clothes, and not too cold, or they wouldn't smooth out the creases. I learned to start with the heavy-weight items first, then gradually moved to the more delicate ones as the iron cooled. After ironing, I would reheat the iron on the fire. It would take me about three hours to finish, as Mum insisted that even socks be ironed. I would finally go to bed around 11:30 pm, only to wake up at 6 am to repeat the cycle.

The only leisure time I was allowed was a Monday evening trip out with some of the girls I worked with to the local Locarno. I had to fight for permission to go out. From my wages of five pounds a week before tax, I had to give Mum two pounds for board. By the time I paid Mum, my bus fare, lunch money for work, and my Mutual cheque, which was a way of buying things in the late 1960s, I had very little left. With a Mutual cheque, you could borrow twenty pounds and repay twenty-one, and back then, you had to be twenty-one to be considered an adult. It wasn't until later that the age of adulthood changed to eighteen, so we were technically breaking the law by obtaining Mutual cheques, but neither the Mutual company nor us teenagers cared much about ages or laws. It was a way to get things we otherwise couldn't afford.

With that Mutual cheque, I could buy a coat, a couple of dresses, a handbag, shoes, and underwear – all for twenty pounds. Then, twenty-one weeks later, I could do it all over again. The day you got to spend your Mutual cheque felt like being an heiress. I would typically have ten bob (now known as fifty pence) left from my wages after paying everything. My Monday night outings cost just that. The only time I couldn't go was if I laddered my tights and needed to replace them. Tights had only just been invented and cost ten bob. You couldn't go to work in laddered tights, as the uniform rules were strict.

So, my ten-bob left over from my wages was just enough for the bus fare there and back, the entry fee, and two glasses of cider, the cheapest drink at the time.

I loved that weekly trip to the Locarno; it was a gilded, perfumed paradise in the ladies' room. Given my home life, transitioning from a dirty, derelict, vermin-infested house to one not much better in terms of overcrowding and lack of money and food felt surreal. We lived in a dismal, post-war city still under reconstruction, while I served as my mother's slave, rarely allowed out. Even though we were now in what was termed the swinging sixties, to people like me, who only saw the magic of the sixties on a black-and-white television, the Locarno ballroom felt like gilded heaven. It transported us post-war teenagers into another world of glitz and glamour, showing us how the other half lived.

The ballroom hosted dance competitions that were televised weekly, displaying professional dancers gliding around to the tango, foxtrot, and other classic dances our parents and grandparents had cherished. The dancers wore incredible flouncy ballgowns made of yards and yards of fabric, while the more exotic Latin dancers donned outfits that, while not as skimpy as those worn today, still provoked shock and outrage among our parents.

The ladies' changing rooms were separate from the actual toilets, necessary due to the size of the ballgowns worn by attendees. The rooms echoed the elegance and exuberance of the dancers. The walls were adorned with the most exquisite silk-like wallpaper, and gold sconces and chandeliers caught the light, reflecting off the golden hues of the wallpaper and making the very walls seem to move. The air was perfumed, with machines scattered about that dispensed shots of expensive fragrance for a mere sixpence. My favourite was Blue Grass. Though I rarely had a spare sixpence, I had filled the machine at work with Blue Grass, so I knew what it smelled like.

For me, with my dark home life, the Locarno was a trip to heaven – an escape from drudgery and a lifeline, just for one night a week. Those ladies' changing rooms transported a common, everyday working girl like me into a world of elegance and wealth that I had only seen on our black-and-white television set at home. Every Monday night, for just three hours, I could escape my life at home.

In stark contrast to today's basic, functional ladies' changing rooms, which are often filled with machines dispensing sanitary items and condoms, the Locarno's changing rooms celebrated a different era. Gone are the silk wallpaper and the perfumes; replaced instead by posters addressing modern issues like AIDS, sexual abuse, and domestic violence – topics that, while present in the late sixties, were seldom discussed.

I can't speak for other towns, but in ours, ballroom dancing eventually fell out of favour as the swinging sixties brought in new dances like the Twist and the Locomotion. Looking back now, we must have looked like a bunch of monkeys, jumping, and leaping about to tunes like "The Locomotion" by Brenda Lee and "The Twist" by Chubby Checker, throwing ourselves around with abandon.

The Locarno itself was a large square room where lads would stand around the walls, watching and summoning the courage to ask one of the girls to dance. Several big staircases led up from the dance floor to a veranda that wrapped around the room. You could sit there to cool off or buy a drink from the bar. Back then, no one asked if you were old enough to drink; it was still a live-and-let-live era, a carryover from the hardships and terror of World War II when you never knew if you'd survive after the bombers flew over.

Much of Coventry was still under reconstruction after being blitzed during the war. The city had been a prime target due to its heavy manufacturing capabilities, producing everything from cars to Spitfires and tanks.

I still dream about that beautiful changing room. After the dances, I would walk to the bus with a couple of workmates who often invited me to their homes for a chat and a cuppa or to grab a bite at the local chippy on the way home. I always had to make excuses; if I weren't home by 10:30, my mother would beat me, and I knew she would stop me from going out again on a Monday.

This was the era of Mods and Rockers, and these gangs would hang out in the cafeteria of our Woolworths, the local gathering spot. As you came up the stairs to reach the staff cloakrooms, you would run the gauntlet of these groups. They were usually well-behaved, though cheeky, often wolf-whistling at any girl who caught their fancy while listening to the piped music provided for cafeteria patrons. My favourite song was Scott McKenzie's "San Francisco", the epitome of what the swinging sixties represented for us shop girls, even though none of us really understood it, coming from a heavily industrialised, blitzed city. Sometimes, these Rockers, clad in leather and sporting long, flowing hair, would cause trouble. I remember one girl getting accosted by a couple of them – it was more high jinks than anything malicious. My mother, who worked nearby, often frequented the cafeteria at lunchtime.

She heard about the gangs and the mischief they caused, and at that time, anyone speaking to me kindly was a rarity. So, when one handsome youth tried to chat me up, I was flattered. My mother, however, was incensed with rage. She put in a complaint to the store, which culminated in the police being called to remove the gangs from the cafeteria. She then took it a step further, demanding a meeting with the store bosses. When she couldn't get her way, she forcibly dragged me from the store, declaring that I was leaving. Just another embarrassing scene my mother caused me.

I wasn't out of a job for long, as I quickly found employment at a small independent store, where I met the girl who would introduce me to my first husband, Mike, on a blind date. This girl, Lucy, had a reputation – she was known behind her back as "Shag Bag" for very good reason. At that point, I was fifteen, going on sixteen. I had been out on a couple of dates with two different boys, but Mike would become my first serious boyfriend.

Shag Bag's boyfriend, Gary, was best mates with my future husband. Gary was around my age, while Mike was over a decade older than us. They lived in the same area and frequented the same pub, making us all part of the same group. The little shop where I worked was one of three owned by a family, and the employees were incredibly cliquey. As the new girl, I was the butt of countless jokes. Once, the manager sent me to the local hardware store to buy sky hooks, and when I asked him what he really needed, he didn't take it well. My punishment for not being silly enough to fall for the joke was to clean out the sludge left in the bottom of the boiler where they cooked the ham joints sold at the meat counter.

Another so-called joke involved the outside loo. If you needed to use it, someone would put a ladder up to the air vent and, while you were in there, would shout down to the person holding the ladder, announcing exactly what you were doing. This was especially embarrassing if you had your period or were taking a number two. I tried to time my visits so that the others were on the shop floor, but one day I mis-timed my visit, and I heard that I was in the loo "playing with myself". This wasn't true, but it left me in floods of tears. In hindsight, I think Shag Bag had set me up with my husband-to-be as a joke; I don't think she expected us to actually get along or become a couple.

I worked at that small store for about six months. On weekends, we would sometimes go out with Gary and Shag Bag in a foursome, primarily because my future husband had a car, and Gary and his girlfriend did not. My husband-to-be was Gary's ride.

Our first night out as a foursome shocked me. At the end of the night, Gary asked my boyfriend to pull over in a lay-by on the way home. Gary and Shag Bag climbed over the roadside fence into a field. I thought they must need the toilet, only to learn from my boyfriend that they were going to have sex. At that time, I didn't know anything about sex; my mother had kept me well in the dark about such matters. She never spoke to me about getting my period at age ten, only instructing me to keep away from boys.

After a short while, Gary and Shag Bag returned to the car, slightly ruffled but seemingly unconcerned that my boyfriend and I knew what they had been up to. As these weekend meetups continued while I dated Mike, it became increasingly common for Gary and his girlfriend to disappear into hay fields or woods at the end of the night for sex. This didn't sit well with Shag Bag, as I had to be home by 11 pm, which cut short her escapades. She became quite nasty with me, telling me I should just tell my mother to "fuck off" and do what I wanted. She had no idea what the consequences of that would be for me.

By then, I had switched my Monday night out for a weekend night out after leaving Woolworths, having to fight with my mother once again just to be allowed out with Mike one night a week on Fridays.

Mike told me that before he met me, he would spend most weekends fishing with Gary, who was an avid fisherman. However, Gary always had to bring Shag Bag along, not because he wanted to, but because if he didn't, she would cause major problems – arguing, fighting, and generally being a real nuisance. It was easier for him to give in and take her with him. Once they arrived at their chosen fishing spot, Gary would start fishing while Shag Bag would moan the entire time, constantly demanding that Gary have sex with her. My boyfriend said that after each trip, he was exhausted from waking up early to fish, then having to spend half an hour on top of Shag Bag before heading home. The number of times they broke up and got back together was unreal. She was not only a sex fiend but also a control freak; when they were out, she wouldn't let him out of her sight. I once witnessed her ask him to fuck her across a pub table in front of a whole crowd of us. To say we were all shocked would be an understatement.

Eventually, after too many breakups, they went their separate ways. Gary then met and married a girl he had gotten pregnant. That marriage lasted a few years and produced two children before they separated and divorced. Gary continued his lothario lifestyle while his ex-wife started seeing a man, got pregnant by him, and, at seven months pregnant, terminated the pregnancy. She told me she couldn't stay with the child's father because he was a drinker and a gambler. That news made me feel sick; we all know that a seven-month-old foetus is preterm and viable. To me, it felt like she had murdered her child.

She eventually married another man, had a boy and a girl, and then split from him years later, ending up alone with emphysema and passing away in her fifties. It was a sad life in many ways.

By the time Gary left Shag Bag, my boyfriend had proposed to me, just before Gary met the girl he would impregnate and marry. I had just turned sixteen at this point, and I was desperate to escape from my abusive mother. Mike, as I mentioned, was thirteen years older than me, had a steady job in a factory working nights, and had his own car, but still lived with his mother. To me, he seemed very mature and responsible, and I thought I was in love.

My mother didn't like the fact that I now had a boyfriend. Initially, I could only see Mike on Fridays, and there was no way she would let me out two nights a week. To spend time with him, I exchanged my Monday night out for Fridays. Despite working full-time, I was still expected to handle all the cooking, cleaning, laundry, and ironing.

At this point, my brother was fourteen, my sister Vicki was thirteen, and my youngest sister Rita was twelve. I pointed out to my mother that it was time for some of her other children to start pulling their weight around the house. Oh my God, that went down like a lead balloon.

Obviously, her star child, my brother, was exempt from all household duties, and my sister Vicki really did not want to give up her freedom to help out. But I was rebelling; I told my mother I would no longer do the laundry or ironing. I made a huge mistake saying that, as Vicki was put on ironing duty, where she proceeded to burn every item of my hard-earned clothes on purpose. I told Mum, who defended Vicki, saying it's not malicious. But when you saw every other family member's clothes were ironed without damage, it was blatantly obvious my stuff was burned for spite.

When out with Mike, I was given a ten o'clock curfew, which made me the brunt of jokes in our social group. But if I did not get home in time, the beatings were hard from my mother. My curfew was increased to 11 pm after Mike spoke to my mother about it.

As I have said before, my sexual knowledge was non-existent; my sister Vicki knew more than me. We were looking out of our bedroom window one night watching all the local teenagers hanging about over the fields that backed onto our garden. I saw a chap lunging up and down on top of a girl. I said to Vicki, "That chap's hurting that girl." Vicki said, "He is not hurting her; they are having sex." I still had no idea of what that actually meant, even though I knew Gary and his birds were having sex; the act itself was very much a mystery to me.

One night after Mike and I had been out, we were sat in my mother's lounge kissing. I was sitting on Mike's lap when he said to me, "I have a hard-on." My reply was, "What's a hard-on?" He was shocked at first; he thought I was having him on until he realised I was serious. He then said, "You had better ask your mum to explain it to you." There was no such thing as sex education classes at school in those days. The next day, I asked my mother, "What is a hard-on? Mike said he had one last night and to ask you to explain."

She looked me up and down and said, "Find out for yourself."

What sort of mother says that to an innocent young girl? I was lucky in the respect that Mike could have taken advantage of me; instead, he explained it to me.

In later years, I found out just how much of a slut my mother had been in the war years and some of the reasons she was the way she was.

My mother and her friends would go into Pool Meadow, our city centre bus depot, fleecing the Yankee soldiers. Mum would get them to start kissing and fondling her while plying them with drink, totally distracting them while the males in her gang crept up behind them, knocking them over the head and stealing their wallets.

She would also ride the army transports along the A45 towards Birmingham, hanging on the ropes tying the cargos down. They would stop at the Malt and Shovel public house, which is still there today, again to engage in sex and the robbery of American servicemen frequenting the pub.

In some ways, it was an era of "live today, because the next bomb could have your name on it", but by the same token, what a despicable way to carry on. On the night of the Coventry Blitz, she and her mates had been running up and down outside Coventry Greyhound Stadium trying to catch the escaped greyhounds set free by the Blitz while bombs and incendiary devices rained down. Such was the mentality of the war years: live today, tomorrow you may not be here.

CHAPTER 5

Mike and I courted for some 18 months. Within this period, my parents moved house to the other side of the city, meaning once again I had to find another job. I found a job at Blummels in Wolston. This site made all sorts: car number plates, steering wheels, and in my section, the inside of cartridges for bullets.

When you walked into my section, you were met by a wave of heat rising from what looked like concrete hedgehogs. Row after row of concrete tunnels with metal rods sticking out of them, through which hot steam was piped. Onto these rods, we would put silver cylinders which we sprayed with a solution of cellulose to cook; this was the inner shell of a cartridge. The silver cylinders, prior to being sprayed with cellulose, would have to be dipped in a solution of grease and sulphur, a very unpleasant-smelling concoction. This stopped the cellulose from sticking once cooked on the hedgehogs. This non-stick solution would soak into your clothes no matter how hard you tried to avoid it. Once the cylinders were cooked, you then had to, without any protective gloves, remove the hot cylinders from the cookers into a duster held in one hand. The reason given for the lack of protective gloves was that if gloves were used, it marked the cellulose cartridge, making them unusable and causing the bullets to stick in the gun instead of firing correctly.

Your hands would be full of blisters. No matter how you complained, you were told to persevere; your hands would harden. All the while, you were suffering not only with blisters but also having to use solvents that aggravated these blisters, like acetone and petrol, which were used to clean the silver cylinders after being removed from the hedgehog cookers and divested of the cellulose inner bullet jacket. Petrol and acetone were the solvents used to clean the cylinders before regreasing and respraying, ready for the second run of the day to be cooked. We were supposed to do two lots of cylinders per day, more if we could. We were paid on piece work, meaning you only got paid for what you produced, minus any flash, another name for damaged or marked cartridges.

My mother was in heaven when I told her I was being paid for piece work; straight away, pound signs rolled in her eyes. She thought she would be getting even more money out of me. Even on the weeks I did make a few bob more, I very quickly learned to say we had had a lot of flash, so no more money than normal that week.

As I paid board, you would have thought it would have covered all my expenses: food, bed, and hot water. I would come home stinking of grease solution but get told I was not entitled to a bath as I had had one the night before, even though my siblings could bathe daily. I was not allowed. My skin started to have problems caused by the sulphur solution I worked with daily. It got to a point where our doctor had to call my mother and tell her to allow me to bathe daily. Usually, when I arrived home from work, my parents, and my sister Vicki, who still lived at home having gotten pregnant at age fifteen, along with her child Sarah, would have eaten their dinner. Mine would be on the stove atop a saucepan of boiling water to keep hot. My routine was to get cleaned up after removing my dinner from the heat and leaving it to cool while I cleaned myself up. I would just be sitting down and raising my food to my mouth when my mother, who was keeping a watch out for her star child coming home from school, would say, "Christine, Ronald's coming; go take his dinner off the stove to cool down for him." As she sat doing nothing along with my sister, why couldn't she get up and do it herself or tell my sister to do it? The first time I actually said, "No, I'm eating my dinner", I don't know who was more shocked – I had actually stood up to my mother. She looked at me with a stare that I knew from previous experience usually meant a beating, but for some reason that day, she looked away, telling my sister to go remove Ronald's dinner from the stove. Looking back, I think that's when she realised, I was ready for her. Even though I had not realised it, my demeanour that day must have given her pause; the worm had turned.

After that day, even though my mother still tried to hold me down, I fought back. The next time she tried to hit me, I gave her a hard slap back. She never raised her hand to me again. From that day forward, I had more freedom.

It was just after this last physical fight that Mike and I set a date for our wedding. I was seventeen years old at that point. My mother did not want me to leave home – not because she loved me, but because she would lose my income. I told my mother if she did not sign a letter to the Vicar agreeing to my marriage – the age of consent had not long changed from twenty-one to eighteen – that as soon as I turned eighteen, I would marry anyway. In those days, young women did not leave home unless it was to go to university or marry, and the age-old saying stood: you made your bed, you lie in it.

In other words, if it all went wrong, there was no going back home. And in my mother's case, that was definite, as by standing up to her, I had, as she told me, burnt my bridges.

Mike and I got married in December; there was snow on the ground. We had relatives and a few friends attend our wedding reception, which was at my mother's house. Mike and I had paid for all the food and drink, with no help from my parents.

My sisters were my bridesmaids. Rita, in particular, loved being my bridesmaid, but as I was leaving the reception that night, she broke down crying. She did not understand I would be visiting home from time to time; she thought she would never see me again. I was concerned for her, as just prior to leaving Elkington Street to move into my parents' present home in Shellon Close, Earnsford Grange, she had started to run away from home, with the police one time bringing her back from Manchester. At that time, she was still at school. Now she was of an age where the police would not bring her home; they did not want to get involved. While I had been at home, I still looked out for her; that would no longer happen.

Mike and I had been looking for a house but had found nothing. By this time, Mike had left his mother's house and was renting a room privately from an old lady Gary had put him in touch with. This lady had rented to couples previously. She told Mike that after meeting me, once we married, I could move in as well, giving us an opportunity to save for our own home. Best laid plans, and all that.

Prior to moving in, while I was visiting Mike one day, her family arrived, and all hell broke loose as she accused her son of stealing a big china platter, which she said was an antique. Her son was raging, telling her, "Why the hell would I steal a china dish? You have had workmen in here; are you sure one of them has not taken the platter?" Without pause, the old lady flew to the door, calling to the workmen who were outside, telling them, "I need to speak to your foreman", who subsequently arrived. The old lady was raging at the foreman; the poor man was stunned. He told the old lady, "Mrs, you are accusing my men of a crime; you had better be absolutely sure of this accusation." At that point, the old lady's son, who had been searching the kitchen, came to the door, apologising to the foreman, telling him, "It's okay; I have found the platter among a pile of old newspapers in the kitchen." The old lady rounded on her son, saying, "Well, you must have taken it and just snuck back into the kitchen!" (Odd, very odd!)

No apology from the old lady to anyone; that should have been a warning to me. Hindsight is a marvellous thing, but at that point, the old lady had always been okay with me.

After our wedding, we moved in together at the old lady's house, spending our wedding night there, where it became clear I was not wanted, but Mike was. As I came downstairs on our wedding morning, she refused me entrance to the kitchen or the upstairs toilet, telling me I could only use the outside toilet. I was not allowed to cook a meal in her kitchen; it was very uncomfortable. At that point, I had no idea why she had turned on me, as prior to the wedding, she had been sound with me. We had wed on the twentieth of December, which was lucky, as it meant I only had to suffer this regime for three days until the old lady went to stay with relatives for the Christmas period, leaving Mike and myself alone in the house. It had not affected Mike as much as me, as he worked nights, so he was asleep all day and at work all night, while I was just sat there all day while Mike slept, not being able to move about the old lady's house unless desperate for the toilet. I had to venture downstairs to use the outside loo, as I had been barred from using the upstairs loo. In the hours in between, I sat in silence on a chair in our rented bedroom so I wouldn't wake Mike up or disturb the old lady, who had effectively banned me from moving around her home. I had nowhere to go, no friends I could visit for the day; at that time, I was not working, so I was stuck.

I had tried to explain my situation to Mike, who I think really thought I was exaggerating, as the old lady thought the sun shone out of Mike; so, when he was around, her behaviour towards me was totally different.

The old lady left the house on the 23rd of December, returning on the 27th of December. During the period she was away, I had such a sense of relief. Mike and I were not in much while the old lady was away, as we did the normal Christmas stuff, like visiting various relatives, actually staying overnight on the 26th of December at Gary's house after a Christmas party, returning to the house just after the old lady had returned home.

I was floored upon entering the house, as the old lady flew at me, blaming me for damaging her table – a table I had never actually touched in all the time I had been in her house. She told Mike that he could stay, but his wife must leave. At that point, Mike realised I had not been exaggerating. While the scenario was playing out, the old lady's son, whom she had previously accused of stealing her china platter, turned up, assessing the situation. He told his mother to calm down, explaining to us that his mother was actually not completely right in her mind – an illness we now know these days is dementia. Mike said fine, went upstairs, collected our meagre belongings, and we left. We spent two very cold, miserable nights sleeping in Mike's car in deep winter, until a chap that Mike worked with, who was a farmer, offered us the end of his farmhouse, consisting of a bedroom and our own lounge, sharing the kitchen and bathroom of his farmhouse in New Arley.

This farmer did a couple of shifts a week at Mike's factory to gain some extra cash – why, I don't know, as from what I saw at the farmhouse, money was not a problem. But then, who knows?

Mike and I moved into his home that day. The farmer's wife, Minnie, who was a lovely woman, made me feel at home. The lounge we rented from the farmer was heated by a coal fire, which I had to light each morning. Our bedrooms were directly above this lounge but had no heating, so even though it was freezing as it was deep winter – and in those days, some fifty years ago, winter was usually very cold with deep snow, not like the warm winters we have these days – it was a lot better than sleeping in Mike's car.

Even if the bed we had in our room sagged in the middle, it was fine with just me in it when Mike was at work at night. But on weekends, when he was home, we rolled together into the middle; there was no way to avoid it. The springs were non-existent; the weight of both of us was too much for the springs. I can still feel the backache it caused to this day. But nevertheless, it was still far better than a car to sleep in.

Minnie told me that as we were sharing her home, she expected me to help with cleaning, obviously keeping our rooms clean. We sorted a rota between us to clean the bathroom and kitchen, which was fair enough. She also taught me how to boil a black pudding for dinner, something I had never done before. As Minnie said, if you fry it, they are too greasy. The first time I tried to do one, all I ended up with was blood water. Minnie told me, "You must have pricked the skin. Once the water gets in, it will revert to the blood it's made from." I never thought of that, but it was a lesson learned.

The farmer would come home from the factory with Mike in the morning, feed his cows, and milk them, then go to bed. The cows were very wary of us; Minnie said it was because we were strangers.

Minnie once took me to the cattle market with her in Rugby, where I was appalled to see whole herds of cows, which Minnie said were bred out so they would be sold and made into beef burgers, being too old for any other purpose. To this day, I cannot eat beef in any form, as all I can see when I look at it is those poor cows in the Rugby market trying to console each other by wrapping their necks around each other. And they say animals are stupid. If you had watched those poor cows, you would have seen the knowledge and fear of their impending doom in their eyes. Actually, I eat very little meat – some chicken every now and then, mostly fish. I think I can stomach chicken, as my mother, when we were young, kept chickens, as told in my first book, effectively desensitising me to their slaughter.

When we moved into the farmhouse, we had our name down on the council waiting list for a property. Some three months into our stay at the farmhouse, we were offered a council flat – it was a top-floor one-bedroom flat in Stoke Aldermoor. In those days, if you did not take what they offered, no other offer would be given. Mike and I viewed the flat; it seemed fine, so we gave notice to Minnie and her husband and moved into the flat. All we had was a bed taken out on hire purchase from the good old Mutual and a carpet, also from the Mutual.

Prior to getting married, like most girls in the 1960s, I had been saving items for my bottom drawer, the term us girls used for items needed for married life. Most of mine had been saved using Green Shield stamps, now known as Argos. You accumulated Green Shield stamps in various ways, the best way being to shop at Tesco, as its founder, Sir Jack Cohen, had linked his stores to the scheme, not only allowing shoppers to get dividends this way but ensuring Tesco became a roaring success. Green Shield had a catalogue of items you could save for, so at least we had plates, cups, cutlery, and bedding. We bought a second-hand gas cooker; another thing people are banned from doing these days; it is all health and safety now. In the sixties, it was still very much a live-for-today, for-tomorrow-is-not-promised society.

Now we were back in the city. Mike continued with his night-time factory job while I obtained work at the local cinema, the Gaumont, another listed building now turned over to student accommodation in Jordan Wells, Coventry, which is now the main hub area of Coventry University.

I worked on the counter in the cinema foyer, selling sweets and drinks, taking turns to do the ice cream run in between films, where you went into the screen with a tray full of ice cream and, in the interval, cinemagoers would line up to buy an ice cream from you. Both of us were on pretty poor wages, just about making ends meet. This was when I realised a lot of Mike's wages were being spent in bookies and pubs, leaving very little left over. That bit left over, when asked, he could not account for. As a young couple, I wanted us to be able to go out once a week; with no spare cash, we couldn't, especially as the flat we now lived in we soon found out was uninhabitable during the winter months, with black mould covering all the walls in the bedroom. It was while Mike was on nights that I had woken up to find my pillow, which rested against the bedroom wall, soaking wet. At first, I could not understand why until I realised there was water running down the walls. These flats have since been demolished, but at that time the council did not want to know, telling us to install storage radiators – damn cheek. As we could not use the bedroom in the winter months, we had to move our bed into the living room. What was a one-bedroom flat became a bedsit, so once again I found myself living in what was effectively a hovel. As such, an evening out or a day trip now and then would have been a break to salve my soul and a welcome respite from a black mould-infested hovel. My dad, who worked for the British Oxygen Company, which is still on Terry Road to this day, asked me if we would like to go to his Christmas works do, telling me he would pay for our tickets as a Christmas gift. I was thrilled. When I told Mike, he was less than pleased, saying we can't afford it. My reply was, "Well, Dad's paying; all we have to do is buy a drink when we're there." Mike begrudgingly gave in. On the night of the do, my dad, my mum, my sister, Mike, and I all turned up at my dad's workplace to board a coach laid on by the company for the event. Once on the coach, one of the office girls made her way down the aisle of the coach to speak to the manager, while wearing a very short skirt. As she bent over to speak to him, Mike made a comment to the chap sitting across from us to the effect of wanting to shag this girl. I was mortified that my husband was making it obvious he had no respect for me while making lewd comments about another woman, making the event I had been so looking forward to suddenly become horrible, and that was only the start.

Upon arrival at the event, we were given table numbers for our places, and the girl Mike had made comments about on the coach was at our table. Even though I had by now told Mike that what he had done was unacceptable, he continued to act as if he was on his own, following this girl around and harassing her. My dad confronted Mike, giving him what for, and after that, he behaved for the rest of the night; but my night was ruined. The next day, my sister came to see me, telling me she had something to share about Mike. She did not want to upset me but told me I needed to know that at the Christmas do, Mike had propositioned my sister, telling her he wanted to shag her. My sister told him, "You're married to my sister, not me." She also told me that she had known for a while that Mike played away from home, as her boyfriend had seen Mike out with another woman. This explained his lack of cash and also explained why, when I asked to be taken out, his usual reply was, "Sorry, I am meeting my mates tonight." I confronted Mike, and he did not deny anything. Sadly, this is when that old saying "you made your bed; you lie in it" came home. After my sister's talk, I approached my mother, asking her if I could return home for a while – something I really did not want to do but had nowhere else to go. Not only did she quote that old saying to me, but she also confirmed she had known about Mike's side woman for a while. So, with no recourse but to try and save my marriage, I returned to Mike, having several long arguments about saving our marriage. One of the issues Mike blamed for his behaviour was our lack of spare cash.

Not long after this event, my dad got Mike a job at British Oxygen with more money, working day shifts. This also gave Dad a chance to keep an eye on Mike's behaviour while at work, and I obtained my job at Crown Wallpapers, where I became a manager until the company started to close shops. While my money was better than the cinema job, it still was not great. It was while working at Crown Wallpapers that I took the part-time job at a Trophy Tavern pub and restaurant, a national chain no longer in our city; it's now a Wetherspoons. Even though we now had extra income, Mike still persisted in blowing money on bookies, alcohol, and women. By this point, I was twenty-two years of age.

CHAPTER 6

The pub job opened my eyes in a lot of ways. It was a great atmosphere working in a place where people were always happy, enjoying themselves and life, reminiscent of the times I had spent going with my then workmates to the Locarno in my teens.

At the wallpaper shop, we knew our jobs were in peril due to the surge in the big warehouse shops, such as B&Q, coming along, where they sold everything needed to decorate and re-modernise your home in such quantities that it was much cheaper to go to those shops rather than ours, which just sold wallpaper and paint. We ran a home deliveries service from Crown Wallpapers; these deliveries were done by part-time drivers who were all firemen. These firemen worked four on, four off shifts in the service, and during their four off days, they did part-time jobs such as our deliveries.

We had three regular firemen servicing our shop's deliveries; one of them took a fancy to me, and to be fair, I reciprocated. He was married with a child, but I was now at the stage in my marriage where I knew it would not last. I had been with Mike for some six years by now, from age fifteen, and married for nearly five of them. His betting and boozing had gotten to me, not to mention his womanising. His personal hygiene was non-existent, which was a massive turn-off for me, and our sex life was over. To be fair, looking back, I had kind of outgrown him. When we married, he was so much older than me that he seemed a safe haven – an escape from my horrible home life – but as I aged, I realised more and more just how shallow he was. His intellect was also not great. You only find out these things when you live with a person full-time. It got to a point with my fireman where he asked me if, on my day off, I would like to go out driving his route for deliveries. Using the excuse "to see how home deliveries worked", I accepted. While out driving with him, he asked me if I would like to go for a drink, which we did. Inevitably, one thing led to another, and we ended up kissing. Things proceeded from there; eventually, we ended up in bed together. Both of us knew it was a fling, but by now I had given up on my marriage completely; it was just a matter of time until I left Mike. To be honest, I do not think Mike was that bothered; he had given up years before me, so why should I worry?

The affair with my fireman went on past the birth of his second child. On the night his wife went into labour, he had turned up at the pub where I was on shift, waiting for me to finish work, taking me to his home for sex, which, when I think back, was really bad on both our parts. If I had been his wife, just having given birth to his child, and I found out he had left me after labour to shack up with his mistress, I would have murdered him. Looking back now, yes, it was bad, but given my life, I was doing my own thing after a life of abuse and misery from my mother and my husband's gambling, womanising, and drinking. My attitude at that point was that no matter what, I was going to enjoy myself. Enough of penniless toil, drudgery, and trying to conform to what other people wanted me to be.

It was not long after the night of his child's birth that we were all given notice at Crown Wallpapers, and both remaining Crown wallpaper shops in our city were closed down. This also ended my affair with my fireman. I still had the part-time pub job and managed to pick up more hours at the pub; this also gave me a different outlook on what went on during different shifts at the pub.

In those days, the pub had two restaurants and bars – one upstairs and one downstairs. The downstairs one had a slightly different menu than the upstairs, catering more to the everyday Joe, while the one upstairs catered to businessmen and the manager's cronies.

The manager was a chap named Ken Greenwell. He was also an area manager for Trophy Taverns. He was a real letch; in fact, most regular customers called him Lecherous Ken. We called him Gee Baby after a popular song of the time, which he found quite funny. By calling him Gee Baby, us girls could usually get away with murder if we did so with a smirk.

He lived at the City Arms with his wife Beryl, who had been brought up in the pub trade, her dad having run a city centre pub for many years. This is where she had met Ken Greenwell when he got a job as a barman at her dad's pub, which was situated in the Burges, a main street in Coventry city centre. This pub is still there today, although it has been renamed and modernised to fit in with our city's new student-popular image.

Ken Greenwell and Beryl had rooms above the City Arms – very basic but liveable. The management strata was Ken Greenwell and his wife Beryl, who only ever came downstairs on a Tuesday when Ken had his day off.

Then there was a downstairs manager, Richard Harbour. Ken Greenwell called him a "no-balls prick" or "Jew Boy" behind Richard's back (as Richard's heritage was Jewish). Richard's wife, a professional model, was the cover girl for all Trophy Taverns advertising, her photographs appearing on the front of menus and all other advertising materials for the chain. Richard was separated from his wife; being a model and very pretty, she had attracted the attention of the Managing Director of Trophy Taverns, with whom she was having an affair, leading to Richard and his wife's separation. Richard had been told that if he didn't rock the boat, not only would he keep his job but would also be promoted to a higher position within the company. At the time I knew him, this was still a very raw subject for Richard; it kind of parodied the film that came out in the nineties, Indecent Proposal, with Demi Moore.

On occasions, the head of the chain would turn up at our pub, as was usual for various inspections, bringing his mistress with him. On such days, Richard would be given the day off, no good rubbing his nose in it. What Richard did not know was that on those days, Ken Greenwell took great delight in calling Richard a 'no balls prick' because of the situation with Richard's wife and the head of the chain having Richard's wife as his mistress. After I left the City Arms, Richard moved to New Zealand, where he still is to this day. While working at the City Arms, Richard had a couple of relationships with members of our bar staff, and one of his bar staff girlfriends got pregnant. She did not know who the dad was – Richard or her husband. It turned out to be her husband's, so she left once the baby was born. Richard again got involved with a member of bar staff. This woman was head over heels for Richard; her name was Pat. She wanted Richard to marry her, but he was not free. Even if he had been, he told me Pat was okay for an illicit fling, but he would not marry her.

Years after leaving pub work, while I was doing promotion and merchandising work, I bumped into Pat at an event held for publicans. It turned out she had met another chap in the pub trade; he ran a pub over Birmingham way, and he married her. So, she had, in effect, got what she wanted – a pub of her own.

On these inspection days for the City Arms, not only would the Managing Director of the chain be in attendance with his mistress, but also Ken Greenwell's boss, the area manager for the Midlands, and his mistress, who was the receptionist at Coventry & Warwickshire casualty department. She still lived with her husband, who was fully aware of her affair, especially as she had a child with the pub chain's Midlands area manager. I do not know if his wife knew of the affair or the child, but most weeks they would turn up at the City Arms for a meal, sometimes with their child and most times with his mistress in floods of tears, usually over the fact he wouldn't leave his wife for her, even after she had given him a son.

Ken's mistress was a girl named Vera Shulko. She ran the upstairs restaurant and bar; her origin was Russian. However, she was not Ken's only bit on the side – he had one in most of the pubs he covered. So not only was he covering pubs, but most of the pubs' female bar staff with his body as well, some of them even still visiting him at our pub from time to time, which Vera really did not like.

Beryl, Ken's wife, was really under the thumb, putting up with all his mistresses and being confined to that upstairs flat six out of seven days a week. Beryl did all the bookkeeping for the pub, handling thousands of pounds in money every day. She also did all the personnel work and all the ordering for the pub.

On a Monday night, Vera would raid the kitchen, taking steaks and salads – anything she needed for her and Ken's day, which they spent together at her council flat, for which Ken paid the rent. He also furnished it, paying for everything it contained, even down to the TV licence. Vera really was the ultimate kept woman. Vera once told me a wife took a man for better or worse; his mistress just took him for the better. That was reinforced by all the jewellery Vera owned, given to her by Ken for every little event. Vera wore several rings on every finger; she took great pleasure in telling me Ken had a friend who was a jeweller in Nuneaton, where Ken would take her, giving her carte blanche to pick whatever she wanted. Each visit – be it a birthday or just a "sorry" for whatever slight Vera experienced daily in her dealings with Beryl, imagined or not (mostly imagined) – Vera took great delight in flaunting her jewellery not only to us bar staff but also in front of Beryl. What made me laugh the most was that while Vera was getting her gifts from a Nuneaton jeweller, Beryl was getting pieces from the really posh jeweller just up the road from the City Arms, costing three times what Ken paid for Vera's gems.

It is so expensive running a wife and a mistress, but when Ken eventually passed, he left over half a million to Beryl in his will; not even his mistress of the time got a penny. As time went along, Vera was telling Ken Greenwell she wanted him to leave Beryl and marry her. There was uproar over that. When I went in to do my shift at one stage, Ken had me ringing around estate agents looking for flats he could rent to move in with Vera – a ploy, as Ken had no intention of leaving Beryl. With hindsight, Ken was quite clever making me do that. As Vera would ask me what I was doing, I would reply, "Ken's got me flat hunting on your behalf." That would make

Vera keep off Ken's back for a bit. When I found a flat that met all criteria, Ken would take Vera to see it but always found a problem with the property. After a short while, Ken had me stop flat hunting, and Vera never questioned me about it, so I assumed he had come up with another delaying tactic to keep Vera happy.

When Ken was off, Beryl would descend downstairs from the flat she shared with Ken to run the upstairs bar and restaurant. It was like watching a butterfly emerge from a chrysalis. Beryl sparkled, enjoying the company of her few friends who always turned up when Ken was absent.

One of these friends was a chap who supplied the pub with chips for the restaurant. He was really friendly with Beryl, so much so that it was rumoured they were having an affair. If they were, fair play to them; Beryl deserved some love and companionship because she sure did not get it from Ken. With what Beryl had to put up with from Ken, who could blame her?

But none of us ever saw any signs of inappropriate behaviour between the chip man and Beryl that suggested they were having an affair.

Beryl was so under Ken's thumb that she could not even come downstairs during a normal day when the pub was open. In fact, on a couple of occasions, I had taken a phone call on the internal house phone from Beryl asking to speak to Ken. He would reluctantly answer, then instruct me to prepare two drinks, which he paid for and took upstairs to Beryl. She was not even allowed to come downstairs for a drink.

People said she was an alcoholic; if she were, she would have been ringing down all night, every night. In my three years of working there, doing five shifts per week, Beryl only ever rang down twice for a drink, and I never saw her intoxicated on the Tuesday nights she ran the pub in Ken's absence. In fact, she only drank lemon and lime.

Ken was such a jealous and controlling person. He would, on occasion, turn up at the pub on his Tuesday night off, leaving Vera, his mistress, for a short period of time, to stand glowering at the end of the bar, making it blatantly obvious he wanted all of Beryl's friends to leave. Not even speaking to his wife, it was a really uncomfortable situation for everyone in that bar, staff included.

He would not move or speak except to ask me for a drink. All of Beryl's friends would be glancing across at him, eventually giving their goodnights to Beryl and leaving early to escape the situation.

Beryl had no life at all.

On one such night, after all of Beryl's friends had gone, Beryl turned on Ken. They had the row to end all rows. Good for Beryl. The next day, when we all turned up for our shifts, we were greeted by the sight of Ken in his dressing gown, opening the pub to let not just us in, but the cleaners, who should have been in two hours prior to us, which was a job Beryl usually did while Ken slept or was at Vera's. It turned out that after their row the previous night, Beryl had packed her bags and left.

Vera had been quite happy Beryl had gone, as she thought it would mean she would become the publican's wife. She did not reckon on the fact that Ken was quite happy for her to stay his mistress, as it gave him carte blanche to carry on his lecherous life with his other side woman. Knowing Beryl was his anchor at the pub, he did not want Beryl to leave.

I do not know exactly what Ken had to do to get Beryl back, but back she came, and things changed once she was back. Ken was still the front man in the pub, but it was obvious Beryl was the power behind the throne. Vera had been furious, but even she did not flounce about in quite the same way as she had done prior to Beryl's leaving and subsequent return.

At the back of the bar was kept a tab where Ken's bar bill was totted up. On occasion, when Ken was out of the pub in his area manager role, Vera would get herself a drink, telling us bar staff to put her purchase down on Ken's bar tab. After Beryl and Ken's ferocious row, where Beryl had packed her bags, Vera was no longer allowed to add to Ken's bar tab.

Prior to the Beryl event, Ken had had Vera's flat re-carpeted. Vera came into work after the Beryl event, telling us that Ken would not get her hallway at the flat decorated, as Beryl had put her foot down.

Vera had, as I have said, numerous rings, all bought by Ken, that she would brag about and their cost. Just after the Beryl event, it was Vera's birthday. Ken took her to their jewellers to purchase the usual birthday ring, but on this occasion, he had a spend limit – another Beryl effect. Vera was incensed, especially as Beryl made a point of coming downstairs on Vera's birthday to flaunt a huge diamond ring Ken had bought her that day!

He could not run the pub without Beryl, so it was decision time: the pub and Beryl, or Vera.

Vera lost. Things continued between Ken and Vera for a while. I think at that point Vera was waiting for Ken to reassert himself with Beryl back to the way he had been prior to Beryl leaving, but it became abundantly clear Beryl had something over Ken. He could only push Beryl so far.

Next thing we knew, Vera was leaving. As the time drew nearer for Vera to leave, Ken was overheard asking Vera, "Would you like a drink? Soon you will not have me to buy them for you."

We all thought this was just another ploy to get Ken to leave Beryl and that Vera would not leave, but it turned out Vera had actually got herself a job in the town centre as a manageress of a ladies' clothes shop, so leave she did. I do not know quite how it worked, but Ken was still going to Vera's on his usual Tuesday night off.

Usually, before Ken left, you could hear Ken and Beryl arguing. Then we all noticed Ken's Tuesday night outings started to become fewer, so it appeared out of sight, out of mind was transpiring as far as Vera was concerned.

One of the waitresses, Diane, with whom I had become quite friendly, kept up her friendship with Vera, meeting Vera regularly for coffee and gossip.

It turned out that Vera had changed her affections to a chap named Mike who had been a regular customer at the pub for years. Mike and his friend Eddie were part of Ken's crew – this crew assembled regularly on Saturday nights when Ken would hold audience, buying them all a meal.

Although Ken never paid for anything at that time when deliveries came in for the restaurant, unlike today's restaurant supplies, all being cut, weighed, and even prepared in some cases on delivery. In the 1970s, chefs did all the prep work themselves; all the chicken came in with spare cuts to make the weights up to those shown on the menus. What customers did not know was that their portions when served were all underweight, as the spare chicken sent in to make weights up were being diverted to Ken's pocket for his Saturday night audience meals. The crew that Mike and Eddie consisted of were local businessmen and their wives, girlfriends, and mistresses. It makes me laugh now when I think back to that crew, as it seems it is not today's footballers who coined the phrase WAGS, but actually, it was the publicans of the early 1970s.

On one occasion, Diane and I missed the staff taxis home. In the seventies, pubs still provided staff taxis home. Mike offered us both a lift; we thought we knew him, and he was safe to go home with as we both lived in the same area.

We both got into Mike's car. As he was driving, Mike asked us if we would like to go for a drink on the way home at a pub he knew. We didn't think anything of it and agreed. After a couple of drinks at the pub, Mike said, "Why don't you girls come back to my flat? It's only around the corner;

we can watch a film and have a few more drinks in comfort." We both agreed and off we went. At Mike's, he poured us a drink. I only had a soft drink as I was a bit tiddly and not being a heavy drinker. Mike was trying to urge me to have an alcoholic drink; he seemed unhappy I was refusing alcohol. Diane was by now three sheets to the wind, her choice not mine. As soon as the film started, I was shocked to see it was a porn film – something I had obviously heard of but never seen. It made me really uncomfortable, especially as Mike and Diane started getting really into it together, kissing, fondling, and within a few minutes, clothes started coming off.

At that point, I stood up, making for Mike's telephone. Remember, this was the seventies – no mobiles in those days. Mike paused in his disrobing of Diane, asking me, "Where are you going? Are you not going to join us?" I really did not know what to do, replying, "Sorry, I am out of here. What you do is up to you." Mike said Ross, his then-girlfriend, would by this point, when watching porn, have had all her clothes off and be screwing him. Shock. My reply: "I am calling a taxi," which I did, leaving as soon as I put the phone down. As I left, Diane was on top of Mike, screwing away.

Oh my God, lesson learned: do not ever take an offer of a lift from a pub customer, no matter if you think you know them; you really do not.

The next day at work, Diane was so blasé about the whole situation, telling me I should have joined in. I reminded her that I was a married woman, albeit in an unhappy marriage. However, by this point, yes, I had been in an affair with my fireman, but group sex was not my thing.

Whenever Mike came into the pub after that, which did not continue for long, I made a point of being polite when serving him but distant. It was not long after that incident that Mike stopped coming into the pub. I thought it was due to that flat event; it turned out it was because of Vera.

After that event, Diane started getting really friendly toward me. With hindsight (a marvellous thing), it was so I would not let on to other staff just exactly what a tramp she was. As if I would talk about such things! I did not want to be classed the same by association.

Diane lived in a bedsit; we would arrange to meet up for coffee, sometimes going out with others for a night out or to the city centre nightclubs after finishing our shift at the pub.

I knew Diane was in a relationship with a married businessman who kept her. What I only found out as we proceeded into our friendship was that she was also the mistress of a local taxi company owner who just happened to be one of Coventry city's councillors. All this came to light after I asked her how she could afford to use taxis as often as she did. For example, we would be having our hair done, after which she would tell me, "Can you ring the taxi? Just tell them it's for Diane; they will know who you mean." She never paid for a taxi; no matter where we were or how late it was, a taxi would be dispatched.

Diane and I would meet up at times during days off for various things: coffee, lunch, that sort of thing. I would usually go to her bedsit to meet her. One day, I stood knocking on her door for an age but got no answer, which was really unusual. So I went around the back, no mean feat as I had to scramble over debris, brambles, and all sorts to get to Diane's ground floor window, which I knew she never left open – too easy to access by tramps and hobos – not to mention the basement access was directly in front of Diane's window. Very deep, if you fell in there when trying to climb through the window, you would be seriously hurt or worse. I managed to climb through the window thinking Diane was sound asleep in bed, possibly after one too many the previous night. As I approached the bed, I realised Diane had actually cut her wrists, as congealed blood spilled over the end of the bed onto the floor.

I swiftly ran out of the house, up the road to the nearest phone box. A chap was using the phone; I yanked the door open, pulling him out, gibbering about Diane while ringing 999. I requested an ambulance, leaving this poor chap stunned at the phone box as I sped back to the bedsit. No mobile phones in those days. The ambulance turned up within minutes; the guys took one look, loading Diane swiftly into the ambulance with blues and twos to Emergency, which at that time was Coventry & Warwickshire Hospital, literally two minutes away from Diane's bedsit. Upon arrival, it turned out Diane had only cut one wrist, just missing the tendons, but had taken sleeping pills as well.

Diane was taken to have her stomach pumped, then into surgery for her wrist. The surgeon said she was lucky to have missed the tendons.

I was in pieces, but glad Diane was going to be okay. Diane stayed in the hospital a couple of days, then went back to her bedsit and to work. At work, she acted as if nothing had happened. I asked Diane why she had tried to kill herself; her reply was that Mike, her married lover, had finished with her.

I later found out this scenario of Mike and Diane breaking up had been going on for over ten years. Diane always found a way to get him back, this suicide attempt being a more drastic way.

The next time I saw my sister, I was telling her all about these goings-on. My sister said, "I know who you mean; we were in the same class at school. Small world!" My sister then proceeded to tell me about how Diane would go into school telling all the girls about her love life, aged just fifteen, and how, on one school day in deep winter, Diane regaled her classmates with a story of her previous night's outing with her boyfriend, which turned out to be the same married businessman (Mike) she was still seeing. She talked about how she had had sex with Mike on the snow-covered ground and that her arse had been frozen! Lying in a snow drift whilst having sex, she must have had an arse made of brass or been lying on a sheep. Talk about soggy knickers – yuk!

Back then, in the 1970s, we still had proper winters with deep snow – not like today's winters.

As our friendship continued, the more I found out and saw, the less I liked Diane. Do not get me wrong; I am not a prude, and yes, I was starting to have my own fun. However, there are limits.

My work at the pub continued, and so did my fun, as by now, my husband and I were like ships in the night. We rarely saw each other, what with our shifts and his continued womanising, drinking, and gambling.

The City Arms was the hub for all the policemen in Coventry to gather, no matter if they were on shift or between shifts. Each bar, of which there were two – one downstairs and one upstairs – had what was called a hull-age book where all breakages and spillages were recorded, alongside all the bungs and bribes given to the local police, with no way of tracing back if it had gone down as spilt, damaged, or broken.

By keeping the force sweet, Ken Greenwell was assured of complete autonomy to act and do as he pleased both in the City Arms and outside in his everyday life. I once watched as he beat a customer quite badly for some imagined insult. The poor bloke was badly hurt; if it had been anyone else, it would have been classified as assault at a minimum or grievous bodily harm at best. We staff knew to keep our mouths shut when we witnessed anything going on, as the police did not take kindly to witnesses who may have compromised their bungs and bribes. Not only did you put your job in jeopardy, but you would also find yourself in everyday life being stopped and searched or accused of various crimes when not at work. Softly, softly was key!

In those days, there were four different shifts working in Coventry police, simply termed A, B, C, and D shifts. I had a different policeman taking me out on each shift, usually after work to the local clubs for a drink, as by now I was, as I termed it, after so many years of being held down and abused – both by my mother and then my husband – living my childhood enjoying myself. Let's face it, I was twenty-two years old by this point, held down, told all my life I was no good and would never amount to anything, living with a husband who, quite frankly, did not give a shit about me. So why not enjoy myself like every other person who worked around me in the pub? To be fair, most of the customers would turn up on various nights with their wives and on other nights with their mistresses and girlfriends, some with multiple girlfriends. It always amazed me that none of them seemed to get caught out. So, play commenced. At that point, I was self-assured none of my policemen would ever meet up, all on different shifts and all in separate police stations. One of them, Edward, was an older man in his thirties who I knew trained the younger officers in his station; the rest of my four policemen were all about the same age as me.

Little had I realised Edward not only trained up his station's young officers but had been the main training officer in Coventry until moving to a different position within his station. Edward had asked me if I would like to go to a wedding of one of his trainees, to which I agreed. On the way home in his car, we were pulled over by a blues and twos. As Edward had been drinking quite heavily at the wedding, he really should not have been behind the wheel. The young officer in the police car approached Edward's car, asking for his licence, etc., then realised who Edward was, letting Edward off, saying, "Sorry Edward, I did not realise who you were," allowing a drunken driver who had been driving so erratically to continue, posing a threat to other road users, both in cars and foot traffic – wheels within wheels. Once again highlighting the fact that police will cover up for their own.

Then there was Steve, who sat one night telling me all about how he had beaten a confession out of a suspect. I asked him, "Surely you're wrongdoing that, and the suspect will have bruises?" His reply was, "No bruises; you learn how to beat people with a rolled-up heavy magazine or similar, so no evidence of criminal behaviour by the police."

All my little jaunts out, all my enjoyment of being cared for, albeit by different policemen, continued for some time – nothing heavy, just fun, meals out, drinks, and being sneaked into the police accommodation in our town centre at night for parties that none of the top nobs at the police station knew were happening. If they ever found out, it would have caused quite a few policemen to lose their jobs at the very least. This came to an end when a serious situation arose in Birmingham one night in 1974 when the IRA bombed the Rotunda in Birmingham. All police shifts were called into duty that night, and all four of my policemen came into the pub to see me by chance. I will never forget that night, one because of the serious nature of the situation in Birmingham, where I was due to go the next day to Lloyd House for my police interview to prospectively become a policewoman.

But by the expression on all four of their faces when they realised, I had been dating all four of them at the same time, they had obviously all met up at some point in basic training. They got chatting at the pub, asking each other, "Why are you here?" all of them saying, "I am dating Chris," then all of them coming up to me as I worked to tell me, "You've been found out. We are all going; none of us will be seeing you again." In a way, it is typical of men's mentality that they can play the field, but if a woman dates more than one man at a time, it is a massive no-no.

Remember, this was just after the swinging sixties when anything went; it's not as if I had been intimate with any of them, but I had just had fun with them all.

Hey Ho! Up to them, they all left, and as per usual after they went, and my shift finished along with the other bar staff, we all went into town to a club where

IT'S ALL PRICKS AND BALLS THIS CHRISTMAS, & GIBLET STEW

I found myself another chap to buy me drinks for the night.

Young, free, and wild at that point, but not as wild as the likes of Diane.

CHAPTER 7

Things had started to stabilise at the pub by now after the dust had settled from Vera's departure; however, it left a gap in the management team, which Ken Greenwell approached me about.

He knew I had managed a Crown wallpaper shop; he also knew I was good with the customers, so he offered me Vera's old job. He also knew my marriage was on the rocks, telling me the job came with accommodation if I needed it. That clinched it for me – escape.

It was also around this point in my career at the City Arms that I started to see a chap, Robert. He was a close friend of Ken Greenwell's. Robert and his friend Derick used the pub a few times a week, coming in together, sometimes on business, as both of them had connections with Jaguar. Robert had a top job there, dealing with rich customers who owned specialist Jaguar cars; this was around the time of the E-Type, a car I loved. Derick had his own business, again dealing with Jaguar in a specialist capacity. Ken Greenwell also owned a Jaguar. Both were married; both had girlfriends on the side.

Robert asked me out one night after my shift; Derick was with Robert, and Derick had his current girlfriend with him. So, all four of us went into town for a meal, which was really nice. Robert and I got on like a house on fire. That was it; we started seeing each other two nights a week. One night was after work; the other was my day off, when we would go as a foursome to the Chestford Grange, a big hotel lying between Coventry and Leamington Spa, where there was a nightclub, the 1812, which stayed open really late.

The relationship began to get quite serious between Robert and myself, but I knew Robert would not leave his wife for me. At that point, it was not something I would have wanted. To me, the way my mind worked was I was borrowing Robert two nights a week – a big difference to asking a married man to leave not just a wife but a child as well. Not something I wanted him to do; as I said, this was my fun era.

My training to take over Vera's job had begun, which meant I was hardly at home with the new job hours and my fun hours outside of work. My husband was being very blatant about his new woman, so it came time to go our separate ways. He did not like that at all, which kind of surprised me until I realised it was because he had lost not only my income – which had been allowing him to continue his wayward behaviour – but also there would now not be anyone at his home to pick up after him or cook for him. It seems I had been not a wife but a servant.

Screw that, mate, I am off. Get your side woman to take over, which he did, but that did not last long. She soon left him once she realised, she was to become his next servant. Then there was one who had a child by him. My dad and my husband at this point were still working together. Dad came home one day when I was making a visit home, telling us that "your ex-husband's partner, the mother of his child, had left your ex" but had also left her child with my ex, who did no more than take his own child to social services, telling them, "I don't want this child; you have him".

I later found out from friends we both had that there had been a succession of replacements after me until one, an older woman, who tied him down.

I bumped into my ex at the local shop one day sometime later. We spoke, and I asked him if he was really settled down now with this older lady. His reply was, "Yes, she is too old to mess me about!"

My reply to this was, "It's not the women who mess you about; it is the other way around, but if you're happy, so be it."

At the pub, Ken Greenwell was becoming very flirty with me. As I was now a free agent, I felt it was somewhat complimentary, taking it as a bit of banter, but also felt it was because I was doing a good job.

Then one night, Robert told me he couldn't see me anymore as his wife was becoming suspicious. To be honest, I was upset. Although I had thought Robert was a bit of fun, it seems deep down I had formed quite an attachment to him. So much so, on the next night Robert came in, I made a point of wearing a see-through top to work, totally ignoring him all night, then going off out with the other bar staff for some fun after work.

The next shift I was at work, Robert turned up, telling me he had made a mistake and wanted to resume our relationship, which I was quite happy to do. Derick was with Robert, who had excused himself for a few minutes to visit the gents. While Robert was gone, Derick proceeded to tell me all about how devastated Robert had been on the night I had worn the see-through top and my total lack of regard in Robert's eyes for him breaking up with me. Derick told me, "You played a blinder, Christine."

Robert and Derick were due to go abroad for a business trip. Upon their return, Derick informed me all Robert had gone on about during their trip was how much he missed me and wanted to be with me. Derick said, "Do not tell Robert I have told you all this." It was not long after this that Derick and his girlfriend fell out. His girlfriend wanted him to leave his wife. Derick would not do that. Not only did he have two children with his wife, which were his world, but he actually really loved her.

This is the difference between men and women: men can and do love more than one woman at a time, while women, in general, only love one man at a time. Like Sheldon from the Big Bang TV series says in one episode, men are genetically made to impregnate as many women as possible to carry on their line, while women carry eggs with a use-by date.

My sister at this point was a single mother of one child. Robert had met my sister when he turned up at my mother's house once to pick me up for a date in a pink E-Type Jaguar. God, I felt like the queen that night. Robert asked me if my sister would go out on a date with Derick. My reply was, "I can but ask," bearing in mind my sister was still living with our parents at that point, so she had no kind of life, not only being a single parent but now replacing me as a slave to my mother, albeit not in as cruel a way as my mother had been to me.

Vicki, my sister, jumped at the chance of a night out. I couldn't blame her for that; it had been about four years since she had last gone out on a date or anywhere for fun, to be fair. So, it was arranged; we met up in town, going to the 1812 for a night out. As usual, on the way home, Robert and I drove to our regular place for a kiss and a cuddle in the woods between Leamington and Coventry. Imagine my shock on the way out of the woods when passing by a car parked up with the windows all steamed up, to see it was none other than Derick and my sister, both without a stitch of clothing on.

WOW!

Don't get me wrong; what my sister got up to was none of my business. However, it was the fact it was a first date – something I can honestly say I have never done in my entire life. Again, I am not a prude, but I do have standards. I must know a man first, and only if there are genuine feelings involved will I become intimate with a man.

Yes, while at the City Arms, I had boyfriends galore but only one with whom I became intimate, and that was a long-term relationship with Robert.

My philosophy was that men can have numerous women at the same time and be regarded as a "jack the lad", a ladies' man, but if a woman played the field, she automatically became a slut, a whore, looked down upon not only by men but by her women friends also. That was just pure jealousy on their part, to be fair.

I was determined to have fun; the devil take the hindmost.

At that time, every year, the National Agricultural Centre, which is located midway between Coventry, Birmingham, Leamington, and Warwick, would hold the annual farmers' show – a massive event for the West Midlands. This brought a wealth of business to our area; all the restaurants, clubs, etc., would be packed out for the week the show was on.

While at primary school, they would bus class loads of children out to the NAC to see the show. It was not just farmers that attended but any type of business to try and sell and promote their wares.

They would have food demonstrations alongside farmers showing their stock, flower sellers, etc. On the occasion our school attended, I saw Princess Margaret being driven about in a Land Rover, and the band of the time in 1963 was The Beatles. I am not sure if it was The Beatles I saw playing at the NAC in 1963, but it was manic around the bandstand where the group was playing.

It may well have been them, as the girl whose mum ran our local shop had obtained tickets to the Hippodrome, our local events venue in Coventry, for her daughter to see The Beatles playing there, which was at the same time as the Royal show. The Hippodrome has been gone many years now, replaced by the Coventry Transport Museum.

All I know is it was red-hot – a beautiful day full of fun, away from a day stuck in a stuffy classroom.

Many years later, while working at the City Arms, a few other staff and I visited the Royal Show again, this time old enough to sample the many drinks given away freely by businesses.

Our group consisted of myself, Diane, and her best mate Rogen, a married Irish lady who worked in the upstairs bar and restaurant where Diane and I worked. I always remember Rogen, as on her time off, she would visit the Arms to socialise. Her drink of choice was whiskey and white lemonade. I asked her one day why she always stated "white lemonade", saying lemonade *is* white. Rogen told me that in Ireland, they add caramel to lemonade, so you can get white or brown lemonade.

After we had been at the Royal Show for a while, Diane, Rogen, and I had gotten separated from the rest of our group, ending up in a tent where they had Spanish foods and demonstrations by the makers of sherry.

One of the demonstrations was being done by a chap using a small jug attached to the end of a long-curved handle. He dipped the jug part into a barrel, swinging it into the air in a curve where the contents were decanted into a small glass without spilling a drop. What a skill, and quite the showpiece!

Diane, it seemed, knew these Spanish people very well. What always intrigued me was just how many prominent people Diane always seemed to be on the best terms with. All around the sides of the marquee were floral displays. As it was the last day of the show, the organisers were telling the children they could take the flowers. Diane, being just about four feet tall, asked me to pick her some of the flowers. I thought nothing of it and started to collect some for Diane. All of a sudden, two big Spanish guys were grabbing my arms, shouting at me in Spanish. To say I was shocked and quite frightened was a bit of an understatement. I did not know what I was doing wrong. I pointed at the flowers in my hand, then at Diane, trying to explain they were for her. As I pointed at Diane, I realised she was sniggering at me. Once the guys realised the flowers were for Diane, they let me go. Both of my arms were red where they had grabbed me, leaving bruises the next day.

I asked Diane what the hell that was all about. She replied that only the children should have been picking the flowers; that is why they grabbed me (not as if I were stealing – they were being given away).

She then carried on to tell me as soon as they realised you were picking them for me it was all fine. I was upset as it had really shaken me up; these guys had been quite forceful, as proven by the bruises on my arms the next day. Diane, however, found it quite funny. It was then I realised she had set me up. It turned out Diane was having sex with the main guy in charge of the Spanish exhibit.

All these years later, I now know the reason Diane was so well in with everyone and knew so many people was that she was a prostitute. The number of different people who knew her very well as we toured that Royal show made it blatantly obvious. Plus, as Rogen was by now very tipsy, she started telling me all about Diane, including the fact that the married guy she had been seeing since her school days was, in fact, her pimp. That explained the relationship with her older married man who had groomed her out of school, the councillor who owned the taxi company still providing her with taxis whenever and wherever she needed one, and in later months how she went from living in her rundown bedsit to one of Coventry's most luxurious high-rise private flat complexes, which she admitted to me she never paid a penny for in rent. And why she worked at the City Arms, a prime spot for rich businessmen in the seventies, where she would go with whichever man had been assigned to her. The Spanish guy in charge had been in the City Arms just a few days earlier when Diane had made an excuse for not taking the staff taxi home but going off with the Spaniard instead.

Eye opener!

Diane then told me she was staying at the Spanish exhibit as she was going off with the guy in charge, leaving Rogen and me to our own devices.

Rogen and I left the Spanish exhibit, wandering about the rest of the Royal show. It was thronged with masses of people, and we ended up in a marquee that dealt with drinks for publicans, where Rogen met two reps who serviced the City Arms on behalf of a brewery. I did not know them as they usually visited during a shift I did not cover.

These two stayed with us for the rest of the show, offering to take us for a meal. We accepted. Rogen, by this point, was three sheets to the wind; she had been drinking vodka and coke. Alongside the NAC runs a river, and as we crossed the bridge to get to the reps' car, a group of tipsy people charged across the bridge, knocking Rogen into the water. It was only shallow; she was not hurt but was wet. One of the reps said, "We have T-shirts in the car to promote Colt 45; you can change into one of those."

Once in the car, T-shirts were given to Rogen. I sat in the front with one rep, while the other was in the back with Rogen. I glanced in the mirror only to see Rogen and the rep getting buck naked. My rep reprimanded his co-worker, saying, "For God's sake, there are people about."

We left the show, pulling into a pub along the way where I helped Rogen from the car into the ladies' loo to change, only to be shocked as my rep just walked into the ladies' loo. I said, "You cannot be in here." He laughed, saying, "It's fine, I just brought in a T-shirt for you." I did not need a T-shirt but took it, telling him to wait outside. Rogen by now had changed, so we headed out to the car where Rogen again got in the back with her rep, once again engaging in foreplay. All I could see in the mirror was Rogen's rep sucking her bare breasts.

Needless to say, I asked to be dropped home first, leaving Rogen buck-ass naked in the back of the car with her rep. God knows what happened after I left, but she was a grown woman who seemed to be having a whale of a time.

The next night, my rep turned up at the City Arms asking me if I would go out on a date with him. I replied, "No, thank you." Diane came over, asking me what he was doing there, so I told her, also telling her that Rogen had been very drunk the previous day. Diane told me that's really unusual for Rogen; she can usually hold her whiskey. I said Rogen was drinking vodka and coke. Diane turned on me, calling me a liar. I was shocked, saying, "Hang on a second, what's this all about?" Diane said Rogen only drinks whiskey. "If she drinks anything else, she will have no idea where she was, who she was with, or what she was saying! Did Rogen say anything about me to you?"

That explained Diane's anger and the way Rogen had been carrying on in the back of the car with her rep. Diane was frightened Rogen had spilled the beans about Diane's true profession, which she had. I said Rogen was too tipsy to be coherent and too involved with her rep to be bothered with anything else. Diane then proceeded to tell me my rep was actually married but was a really nice chap, how she had accompanied him on several business trips in the past, and how he had looked after her, bought her dresses, and made sure that when she was drunk, she was tucked up in her bed. I asked her if she usually accompanied reps on business trips. She replied yes, when (Mike) her married boyfriend organised them. So again, reading between the lines, Diane was being supplied to Mike's clients. This situation was the catalyst for Diane, who started to carry out a campaign against me at work. Diane had been quite off with me since her suicide attempt, which I did not understand as I had in fact saved her life, or so I thought.

But then came the realisation that I knew too much and had become a threat to Diane. As I said previously, Diane had been living in a dump of a bedsit right on the main road into Coventry city centre before she got her luxury apartment from her city councillor. While living at that bedsit, Diane had a live-in bloke Monday to Friday (John), a Londoner. John and his workmates were living in Coventry during the weekdays while working in the area; on weekends, he would go back to London, where it turned out he had a wife! Diane knew, but it was a good situation for Diane. John provided for all of Diane's bills during the week, while at the weekends, Diane's married lover provided. There were times when one or more of her providers, for whatever reason, would not be around; they would tell Diane they had work or family commitments.

That was when Diane would return to one of her other options. She was never short of a provider, money, food, or cash; in fact, she literally dripped with designer clothes, good jewellery, and was always having some costly beauty treatment or other, none of which I ever saw her pay for personally. It all went on tabs under various names, just like her taxis.

Then a new girl started at the pub who, when she started, Diane disliked (Jackie). After the Rogen issue, Diane made a point of courting Jackie as her new friend while blanking me. It made it very uncomfortable at work, as with my new position in Vera's place, I had to give Diane jobs to do, liaising with all staff in my new management position. Not great when one member of staff is blatantly giving you trouble and totally disregarding anything she was asked to do by me.

Ken Greenwell asked me what was going on. I told him, and he took Diane aside to talk to her. Instead of making the situation better, it made it worse.

Around this time, Diane and John started to drift apart. There had been an occasion when John had asked Diane to fix his boss Dan up with me on a date. As we were friends at that point, I agreed to go on the date but really did not like Dan.

Dan told me that up to the point of going on a date with me, he had been shacked up with one of Diane's previous friends. He said the friend had become too demanding. The thing was, with these guys, all of the women they were shacking up with in our town were purely for sex while away from their wives and lovers in the smoke. So, if one got too big for their boots, they were kicked to the kerb, and Diane provided another fool to take their place.

I am no one's fool!

On top of that, John had made it plain to me that he fancied me. I made it plain to John that Diane was his woman, not me. Even though Diane could see I was not reciprocating John's feelings, she was still very jealous – not my fault.

The next thing we knew, Diane and John had split. Diane said it was because the contract they were all working on had ended and they had all moved on. Suffice it to say, Diane was gutted, as it meant one less provider for her. The next thing we knew, Jackie had moved into Diane's bedsit with Diane. As I knew from past visits to the bedsit, there was a sofa on which Jackie could have been sleeping.

Diane's vendetta against me escalated, as now she had Jackie as her best friend. Jackie was also making waves at work: little things, snide remarks, not doing jobs I had asked her to do, general nastiness. Obviously, all the other staff who were watching this situation began to experience a knock-on effect, as they were thinking, if Diane and Jackie can do it, so can we, undermining me at every turn. So much so that Ken Greenwell told me if it did not calm down, either myself or Diane would have to go.

I then informed Ken Greenwell of exactly what had been going on; he was not surprised.

A few nights later at work, I was in the ladies' loos when I heard the door open. In came Diane and Jackie, giggling like a couple of schoolgirls, talking about me. I stayed silent in my cubicle. Imagine my shock when Diane told Jackie she had purposely left that bedsit window open, knowing I would climb through it, that she had only cut one wrist on purpose, and only taken a small dose of sleeping pills, knowing just how much was needed to make me think she was worse than she had been, that I was a gullible prick with no balls for letting the situation continue. Her treatment of me was revenge for knowing too much about her private life (I only knew what Diane and Rogen had told me). Diane also said John, her Londoner, had told Diane, yes, he did fancy me, that they had had a blazing row over that fact, at which point John had told Diane I had rebuffed him. Diane was so angry at that point she had picked up a knife and tried to stab

John, catching his hand. John told Diane, "You are a crazy cow, and I am leaving you." Diane said, "Chris knows too much about my many clients," and all the other Diane situations I had witnessed since becoming her friend; at which point Jackie said, "I know Ken is not happy with the situation between all three of us at work."

At which point, they exited the loo, continuing to chat away as they went.

I came out of my cubicle thinking I was the only one in there. So, imagine my surprise when the door next to me opened and out walked Beryl.

My opinion of Beryl was confirmed as she walked over to me, putting her arms around me, saying, "Right, come with me." Beryl took me into her office, leaving me there to return a few minutes later with her husband Ken. Beryl informed Ken of everything she had overheard being spoken about between Diane and Jackie. Ken asked me a few questions, saying, "Right, leave this to me." He then left the office, leaving me with Beryl.

Beryl started to tell me Diane was known for her outside liaisons, not mentioning Diane's connections within the pub. I kept quiet about those, as to be fair, I did not know if Beryl knew of those connections or even Ken. But if he did not, I would have been shocked, as let's face it, Ken really put himself about. After all, not only was he the manager of the City Arms, but he was also an area manager, having some fifteen other pubs under his command. After a few minutes, Beryl told me to go back to work. I made my way back up to my restaurant; Diane and Jackie were still working away. At the end of the shift, we all left. By now, as my husband and I had split, I had taken Ken up on his offer of moving into staff accommodation, which was in the house right next to the Arms.

I had only been in my room about twenty minutes when there was a knock on my door. It was Ken and a few of his crew. Ken asked me if I would accompany them to the nightclub-cum-hotel he oversaw near Coventry, telling me, "As you are now a trainee manager, you really should see the inner workings of the nightclub." I could not really say no, even though I was upset and tired.

Upon arrival at the nightclub, we all went in. I was expecting Ken to be there in a formal capacity, but it became apparent he was there to socialise, buying me drinks and generally chit-chatting. The manager of the nightclub came over to us; Ken introduced me as his trainee manageress. The guy (Shaw) seemed really nice as we chatted. A woman came over talking to Shaw, the nightclub manager. She wore a diamante-encrusted name tag that said Mr Brown.

I asked Ken if she was the wife of the nightclub manager, whose second name I did not know, as Ken had introduced us by first names only.

Ken laughed and said, "No, that's Shaw's mistress. His wife is overseeing the hotel complex. Shaw's wife has no idea Mr Brown is Shaw's mistress, as they are both kept separate from each other, running two different parts of the complex. Even though Shaw's wife does the wages, Shaw's mistress is down on the wages sheets as Mr Brown, who Shaw's wife thinks is the bar's manager here." I was stunned. I said, "Surely they will bump into each other one day." Ken laughed again, saying, "No, one works days, the other nights, and in separate parts of the complex. Mr Brown knows Shaw's wife but not the other way around."

How flipping devious was that!

To this day, I still cannot believe how that situation continued to work.

Among the crew that night was a manager from one of the city centre pubs that Ken oversaw, nicknamed Smithy, who was, it seemed to me, a really nice chap. He was married, and his wife was not with him that night.

The evening progressed, and everyone was having a good time. The nightclub closed about 2 am, at which point Ken and I left. On the way back to the Arms, Ken chatted away about the pub trade, how he had gotten into it, and just general chit-chat. Arriving back at the Arms, I bid Ken goodnight. Turning away from his car, as I did, he grabbed me and kissed me. I was stunned; pushing him away, I let myself into my room, putting his embrace down to drink.

The next morning, my dad turned up at the Arms for a pre-arranged visit as we were going into town together to pick out a gift for a family member. My dad came armed with my favourite childhood dinner he would make – giblet stew, complete with a great big dumpling on top. Dad knew I was in an emotional state at that time due to my marriage breakup. My emotional state was now compounded by Ken kissing me the night before, which I had put down to drink, and the Dianne and Jackie situation. I still had to face Ken that day.

Dad and I talked over the work situation. I did not tell him about the Ken thing. Dad, as usual, was a great comfort, giving me some valuable emotional support and advice. Off Dad went back home, leaving me to get ready for work.

Upon arrival at work, Ken was nowhere to be seen – no Diane and no Jackie. In the back of the Arms was a space where staff would go for a break, out of sight of management and punters – a hidey hole.

You could not see staff in there, but by the same token, staff could not see you. I was early; not a staff member in sight, so I crept up on the hidey hole, eavesdropping on the staff gathered in there. Imagine my surprise to hear them discussing Diane and Jackie, and how the staff knew the pair of them moving in together was more than just a convenience thing. One of the girls, Susan, was relaying a conversation she had had with Diane from the night before. Diane had been telling Susan about how Jackie and her current boyfriend were engaging in full sex on Diane's sofa bed while Diane sat watching from her single bed in the bedsit. Diane had been laughing about how Jackie and her boyfriend were, as Diane termed it, just getting to climax when Diane stood up with a glass of water in her hand, throwing it over the pair on the sofa bed like you would to two dogs in heat. The shock of the cold water separated the pair just like I had watched my mother, as a child, separate two dogs in our street. Jackie's boyfriend had been less than happy, storming out of the bedsit. Diane had been in fits of laughter while regaling Susan with the tale. Diane told Susan Jackie had been left on the cusp of orgasm, so Diane went down on Jackie, finishing her off and bringing her to full orgasm. Susan was warning the other female staff about Diane, saying, "Diane is bisexual; do not let yourselves be caught anywhere on your own with her."

Most of the staff were shocked at the revelations by Susan; I was not. Susan also said it was a waste of time saying anything to management about Diane, "as Ken is a prick with no balls. All he cares about is his love life and other women. Ken says Richard Harbour is a prick with no balls for putting up with the fiasco of his wife's affair with the area manager. Well, I don't know about you lot, but I think Richard has balls of steel, as every time his wife and the prick of an area manager come in here, although Ken tells Richard to take the day off, Richard makes a point of being in both of their faces while they're here, facing them down. Good for him".

I left the area before the staff knew I had been there, going about my routine, and making some noise so they knew someone was about. They all came into the restaurant doing their opening procedures as they did. Diane and Jackie arrived along with Ken from his flat upstairs.

To my surprise, Ken was followed by Beryl, which was unusual to see both of them together. Ken stopped Diane and Jackie, telling them both he wanted to see them in his office. All four of them went into the office, while the rest of us just carried on working, getting the restaurant ready for the lunchtime shift.

A short while later, Ken came back into the restaurant, and Beryl went back up to their flat. There was no sign of Diane and Jackie.

After the lunch shift finished, Ken asked me to go into the office with him. I was apprehensive as it was the first time we had come face-to-face since he had kissed me; however, nothing was mentioned about that incident. He began telling me he had suspended both Diane and Jackie without pay. He had informed them that the issues they had been causing with me could no longer be tolerated. I was blameless, and Beryl had overheard them in the ladies' loo talking about how they had set me up. Upon their suspension ceasing, they would be allowed to return to work as long as they behaved; no further action would be taken against them. Ken said it was the best he could do under the circumstances. To be fair, I was relieved, not only because Diane and Jackie had been caught out, but also because it seemed, as I had thought, the drunken kiss Ken had inflicted on me was just that and soon forgotten. And once again, Beryl was proven to be the power behind the throne.

My training continued while Diane and Jackie were absent. Ken continued to be flirty, but no more advances, thank goodness. Robert and I still saw each other after work and on my night off.

I had booked a day's holiday as an old friend from my Crown wallpaper days, Helen, was coming over to Coventry to see me. She had gotten engaged and wanted me to meet her fiancé. We met up in town; her fiancé was lovely, and I was so happy for her. As the day carried on, her fiancé went off, telling me it had been nice to meet me but that he had to get to work. He kissed Helen goodbye, saying he would see her later. Once he had left, I started regaling Helen with all that had passed since last seeing her. We had a bite to eat in one of the city centre's restaurants, and I then said, "Let's go see Smithy at his pub," explaining who Smithy was and how I had met him.

Upon arrival at Smithy's Pub, he was pleased to see me, making Helen and me very welcome and introducing us to his wife, whom I had not met until then. Smithy's wife was not as nice as Smithy; I found her very rude, to be fair. Smithy sat chatting with Helen and me, buying us drinks when our glasses were empty. The night was wearing on, and I was having a really nice time after all the stress and emotion of the past few weeks . . . Until Smithy went up to the bar ordering us another round, his wife flew across the pub, delivering our drinks and slamming them down in front of us, saying, "Right, that's the last round you will get."

Stunned much!

Smithy apologised, going after his wife; we could see them having words behind the bar. When Smithy came back, I asked what we had done. He said, "Nothing. She is just a jealous woman." I now realise that at that time, in a lot of ways, I was quite naive.

To me, all that Smithy was doing was chatting to a fellow manager and her friend, part and parcel of the pub trade. Interaction with customers is vital in the pub trade, especially as the person Smithy was chatting to was the trainee manager of his area manager's pub. I told Smithy I am really sorry if I have caused you a problem. We finished our drinks and left. Helen gave me a lift back to the Arms, leaving me with an invitation to her wedding.

It was still early in the evening, about 10 pm, so I popped into the Arms for a nightcap before going to my room.

Ken asked me how my day had gone, so I chatted away to him, telling him we had popped into Smithy's pub. He asked me how I had found it; in my naivety, I regaled him with the situation as it had happened, saying Smithy was great but not so much his wife. Ken asked me to explain further, which I did, thinking nothing of it. I was so naive.

A few nights later, a very distraught Smithy arrived at the Arms, passing by me in the corridor and asking me where Ken was. I replied, "In the restaurant."

As I returned to the restaurant, Smithy was having a very emotional talk with Ken. Smithy was almost in tears; he then left.

I went up to Ken, asking what all that was about. I was appalled when Ken informed me that Smithy had applied for a big pub in Ken's area, which had seemed a done deal until my visit to Smithy and my regaling Ken with my night out.

Ken had taken umbrage to the way Smithy's wife had been with me. I was appalled; it felt like I had stabbed Smithy in the back. I tried to reason with Ken, telling him, "Come on, Ken, that's a bit hard, taking it out on Smithy like that. It's not his fault his wife is a jealous woman." Ken said, "No, it's not, but think of it like this: in the pub trade, you and your wife are partners. No matter what happens between those partners in private, it cannot be allowed to impact the customers in your pub. They are, after all, the people who keep you in a job!" Well, to say I was stunned by that was a bit of an understatement, considering how he was with Beryl. On the other hand, I could see where he was coming from. I still felt really bad for poor

Smithy; he had been devastated, especially as Ken had retold to Smithy the exact reason for him not getting that pub. To this day, I hope to God my visit to that pub did not impact Smithy's marriage as well as his promotion. Going forward, I had learned a valuable life lesson: keep your gob shut, think before you speak, or it may cause someone a hard life in theirs.

As the evening progressed, one of the new under-managers Ken had taken on, Slimy, came upstairs to chat with Ken. I was working in the restaurant, taking bookings, and leading guests to their tables. I could see Slimy, as we all called him behind his back, as his personality was just that friendly; but you knew he did not mean what he was saying, just like the worst kind of slimy salesman you ever met. Richard Harbour really did not like him. Richard had warned all of us girls to be on our guard against him after catching him telling tales to Ken about Buzz, the downstairs head barman. Buzz would take home the ends off the big Stiltons we used in the restaurant – not good for anything in the pub – but Buzz would use them to make different meals at home for his family, which was quite a large brood. As bar staff wages in the early seventies were really poor, unbeknownst to Slimy, Buzz had asked Beryl if he could have them. Beryl had agreed; otherwise, they would just have been thrown in the waste.

Slimy was a wet-behind-the-ears kid who thought he knew everything about pub trade. Slimy and Buzz had a difference of opinion over several routines in the downstairs restaurant on how things should have been done (if it's not broke, don't fix it). Bearing in mind that Buzz was in his forties and had been in the pub trade all his life, while Slimy was a really new beginner, Buzz had been proved right about the issues between them. So Slimy began a vendetta against Buzz, always on Buzz's case about the least little thing, picking on Buzz for the smallest issue. Good job Buzz was such a mild-mannered man; otherwise, Slimy would have been without a few teeth.

We then had a new influx of waitresses, one of whom, Joleen, made a beeline for Slimy, flirting and hanging on every word Slimy uttered. Slimy had not been adverse to anything in a skirt prior to Joleen's arrival, but this was a whole new ball game. The next thing we all knew was Joleen was telling other staff what to do, when to do it, and how to do it. Like Slimy, Joleen was a wet-behind-the-ears kid, so as you can imagine, the other staff were not happy. Now, while I was a trainee manager for the upstairs restaurant and was gradually being versed in all pub routines by Ken, the downstairs was Richard Harbour's to run. After a short while – as was usual on Ken's night off, a Tuesday – Richard would come upstairs to help me with the running of the upstairs floor while Buzz and Slimy were running downstairs.

Richard and I were chatting away as it was a really quiet night. Since Vera had left, Beryl did not often come down on Ken's night off anymore, so we were left to it. Richard was regaling me with tales of Slimy, Joleen, and Buzz's escapades of the week. Richard was telling me how he had gone out to the meat locker situated in an outbuilding across the yard at the back of the pub to bring in the needed meat supplies for the restaurant, which was usually a job Buzz did. Buzz had told Richard he had hurt his back getting in the dray delivery that morning, so he couldn't do the meat haul. Richard had trotted across the yard, throwing open the big door to the meat locker. As he did, full sunlight streamed into the locker, highlighting Slimy and Joleen, buck naked in the throes of intercourse against the big chest fridge. Richard was falling about laughing as he recounted the tale, saying, "I don't know who was more shocked, them or me, but I can tell you this much, Chris: Slimy is not a big bloke, and I really don't think any of this week's steaks will need any seasoning at all after the spice I saw this morning in that locker! And there was definitely no brewer's droop to be seen!"

Well, what do you say to that?

I knew Joleen took after Slimy as far as chasing anything in trousers was concerned and that they had an obvious thing for each other, but this was truly confirmation of our suspicions. No wonder Buzz had asked Richard to get the stock from the locker; Buzz knew what was going on out there. Richard said when he came back into the pub, Buzz had been positively gleeful. Now Slimy would have to be careful, as if Ken found out – like with the Diane and Jackie situation – it was do as I say, not do as I do. Slimy would have been out if Ken knew.

What it did do was calm the situation down between Buzz and Slimy as Buzz now had the whip hand backed up by Richard.

A few days later, Diane and Jackie returned to work. Ken had put Jackie on the downstairs floor while Diane stayed upstairs. To be honest, I had some trepidation about Diane's return but was determined she would not get the better of me. I was quite surprised when Diane approached me, telling me she wanted to apologise for her behaviour, which I accepted. But a leopard never changes its spots; I would always be on my guard with Diane. I would not engage in the chit-chat that used to take place after shifts, as had previously happened.

IT'S ALL PRICKS AND BALLS THIS CHRISTMAS, & GIBLET STEW

Jackie and Diane were still sharing the bedsit, but now Jackie was working the ground floor. The upstairs floor began to learn more of the scandals transpiring among the ground floor's staff via the Diane grapevine. It turns out while Diane and Jackie had been suspended, Diane had been frequenting another one of Ken's pubs in Kenilworth, where she had found yet another provider to replace John, her Londoner. This provider was the manager of the Kenilworth pub, which Ken oversaw. What it also did for Jackie was, through Diane's new provider, Jackie had also acquired a new provider, who turned out to be one of the directors of Trophy Taverns, who was, in fact, Ken's boss. Jackie and the director seemed to be getting along famously, and for a change, this one was not married.

One of the new waitresses, Hazel, working the downstairs floor, was of African origin, born and bred in the UK, her parents having come over in the fifties to find work. I had not had much to do with Hazel, but on occasion, if we were short-staffed upstairs, Hazel would work upstairs with us. I found her to be a really nice girl with a good work ethic. One night, Richard came upstairs saying, "I am going to send Hazel upstairs to work; there's a bit of banter going on downstairs, and Hazel is getting upset." I never questioned Richard; I just said, "Fine, send her up." We were very busy, so the extra help was appreciated.

Hazel came upstairs, asking me, "Which station should I work? But please do not put me next to Diane." I asked her why, and Hazel said, "Watch and listen; you will see why."

I left it at that, not wanting to push the girl as she was upset; best to let her calm down.

As the shift progressed, I kept an eye on Hazel as she worked. Hazel purposely avoided Diane at every turn. Then I saw Diane say something to Hazel that made Hazel flinch. I kept observing. Richard came back upstairs, and I asked him what was going on between Diane, Jackie, and Hazel. Richard said, "As far as I can see, a bit of name-calling."

I asked Richard if he had overheard any of the names. He said no. I told Richard to go quiz the downstairs staff, which he did, coming back a while later saying, "Diane and Jackie are calling Hazel 'jungle bunny', 'nigger', 'spook', and any other really nasty name you can think of."

Bearing in mind we are talking about the very early seventies now when this type of racist harassment was not heard of, and if it was, it was very rare.

I told Richard, after shifts are finished, we need to sort this out; it cannot be allowed to carry on.

Richard agreed. Going back downstairs about fifteen minutes later, I saw Diane remove a decanter of salad dressing from Hazel's station, which was weird as it was far away from Diane's station, returning a few minutes later with the decanter topped up. I never gave it a thought until Hazel took the decanter to a couple she was serving, asking them if they would like some. Hazel proceeded to spoon the dressing over the couple's meals. All of a sudden, the couple were gagging. I flew over to them, asking what the problem was, picking up the decanter before any of them could touch it. The couple were looking decidedly green. I tasted the dressing; it was full of liquid soap. Hazel was aghast, telling me she had no idea how that had happened. I told Hazel, "Don't worry; let's sort out this couple first," which I did. We were very lucky the couple had only tasted a very small bite of the dressing; they could have been seriously sick.

I took the decanter away, phoning down for Richard, explaining to him the situation when he came up to me. Diane had purposely filled that decanter with soap to try and get Hazel into serious trouble. Luckily, I had seen Diane remove and return the decanter – not as if she needed to be anywhere near Hazel's station, and Diane's own decanter was visible to me from my vantage point, which was full; there was no need to top up or borrow anyone else's decanter.

At the end of the shift, Hazel was very upset, not only from all the name-calling she was suffering but also from the couple's meal scenario; her nerves were shredded. As the staff collected in their usual corner to have a drink and collate their stations for the shift, Jackie came upstairs to Diane. They were both whispering and giggling to themselves, casting sly looks across at Hazel.

It seemed I was right; the leopard had not changed its spots. Now they were making Hazel their prey instead of me.

Until Richard went over to them, telling them he wanted to see them both in the office, asking me to come along also. Richard proceeded to inform them both their behaviour was not going to be tolerated. Diane never said a word; she knew better. Jackie, however, was full of herself, bragging how her boyfriend, Ken's boss, would not allow Richard to discipline Jackie if Richard knew what was good for him!

Ken at this point was away on holiday for a couple of days. In the early seventies, disciplinaries were done only by pub managers. Richard, although in charge, did not have the power to act on a disciplinary. So, he told them both, "As soon as Ken's back, you are both looking at a disciplinary," letting them go off to catch the staff taxi. Both of them were not due back in for the next three days.

The next day, Diane turned up at the pub asking to speak to Richard. Once again, he asked me to sit in. Diane proceeded to inform us that Jackie was being such a bitch, as she was pregnant with Ken's boss's baby and her emotions were in turmoil. She also said the boss at that time was unaware of the pregnancy and that Jackie and Diane were travelling to the head office to see him to enlighten him to the fact that he was about to become a daddy.

Apparently, Jackie had been trying for a couple of weeks to see her boyfriend but was getting told by his office that he had been called abroad suddenly and was not contactable; in other words, getting the bum's rush. Diane said Jackie was determined to go see him, as Jackie thought he may be unwell or some such, and his office was just covering for him. Richard told Diane there was no excuse for her and Jackie's behaviour. Diane said Jackie firmly believed she was invincible as she was pregnant by Ken's boss. Richard asked, "When are you going to see him?" Diane said, "We are leaving in about an hour."

The next day was really busy on both shifts as the crock fair was back in town, an annual event sited on Hearsall Common, not very far from the City Arms. Not only did the crowds the crock fair drew in mean extra business for the Arms, but after the fair closed for the night, the travellers running the fair and all the roadies would pile into the Arms for a meal, packing out both upstairs and downstairs restaurants. Wow! The money they spent was unbelievable, and they could literally drink anyone under the table. But contrary to popular belief, they were all really nice people. Fair folk have garnered over the years a bad reputation; at the Arms, we never had a second's trouble from any of them.

There was no sign of Diane or Jackie, as they were not due in until the next day. However, one of the fair guys came up to me asking after Diane. I was surprised, telling him she wasn't in until tomorrow; may I pass along a message? He said, "No, I am seeing her while I am in town. She was supposed to meet me after work tonight." I explained she was helping a friend out with a personal issue. He snorted and said, "Oh, you mean Jackie," sneering as he said it, then turned on his heel to walk away. I put my hand on his arm, asking him if I could help him at all or pass a message along when I next saw Diane. He told me, "No, it's okay. I will go to the bedsit and see her."

Richard and I were surprised that the pair of them had not shown up to brass it out with us before Ken came back into work, which he was due to do the next day, or at least that we had a phone call from Ken's boss. If they had turned up, the fair guy would have seen them both, even though it seemed, from his attitude, he was less inclined to want to see Jackie. The shift went ahead without any expected phone calls from head office or any form of communication from Ken's boss. The next day, when Ken was back at work, Richard had apprised him of the goings-on with Diane, Jackie, and Hazel. Ken was less than pleased about the situation; as I have said before, with Ken it was do as I say, not do as I do at work.

That night, as I arrived for my next shift, I popped into the ladies' loo only to bump into Diane. "No Jackie?" I asked. Diane said Jackie was at home and not coming in because she wasn't well. As I spoke to Diane, I could see she was not quite right. I asked her what the problem was; she said she had cystitis but had been to the doctors and was on medication, that she would be fine.

I informed Richard about Jackie, also telling him Diane had not mentioned anything about their visit to head office. We thought Diane had not said anything as Jackie was not in work; to be fair, it was Jackie's business to tell us, not Diane's.

As the evening wore on, the fair people came in for their meals. The guy who had been asking after Diane the previous evening was late arriving; Diane was on the lookout for him. As soon as he arrived, she was all over him like a rash, but to my surprise, he was quite distant with her at first. I took that to mean he was annoyed with her over the previous evening. At the end of the shift, as was usual, all the crew sat sorting out their stations while having a drink, at which point Diane's fair man went over to her. They seemed to be having a bit of a heated discussion. I then saw Diane pull out a pair of nail scissors from her pocket and proceed to trim the fair man's nails over the waste bin by her side.

As she was doing the trimming outside of the food area and over a bin, nothing was said to her. After she had finished, the fair man gave her a kiss on the cheek and off he went.

I went over to Diane and asked her what that was all about. Now bear in mind this fair man was on the grubby side from working fairs all day every day with limited washing facilities. This was the seventies; there were no showers in caravans in those days, just a sink where you had to get water from a standpipe to bring into your caravan to fill your sink.

I must have taken Diane by surprise as she told me, "I had to cut his nails. I don't really have cystitis; my fanny was cut to ribbons while having sex with him from his nails!"

My stomach lurched at the thought. Now I know we had found out Diane was a prostitute; however, how could you go with a bloke who was so damn filthy, whose nails were encrusted with dirt, and who had mauled your fanny so badly with those filthy nails that it had caused you actual cuts to your fanny? Yet she was once again going off with him after work as the fair was leaving that night to travel to Manchester. She would be travelling back the next day to come back into work for her late shift. He was obviously paying her well; all the fair people were minted and dripping with gold jewellery. When you think about all the women, he must be picking up all over the country, dirt-encrusted nails were the least of the things he would be passing to his sexual partners.

The next day both Diane and Jackie turned up at work. Jackie was visibly upset, while Diane had a very sneering expression on her face. Before the shift began, we took them into the office to thrash out the situation with the soap in the decanter. Jackie immediately broke down, telling us she was abjectly sorry for the whole incident. Richard asked her why we had not heard anything from her VIP boyfriend, the father of her child.

Diane had to talk for Jackie as Jackie was incoherent. Apparently, the VIP boyfriend had not been out of the country at all. When the pair of them had got to head office, they had to make a scene to get anywhere near the VIP boyfriend, who had blatantly disavowed all knowledge of his paternity to Jackie's baby, telling Jackie, "Do you really think you're the only barmaid I shag? And do you really think you're the only barmaid who has told me the baby you're carrying is mine? On your bike, don't let the door hit you in the ass on the way out."

So now Jackie was without her VIP protector. More importantly, she was in deep shit over the Hazel issue, and Ken was positively gleeful that his VIP boss was having nothing to do with Jackie. What made it worse for Jackie was the fact she had been so uppity with us over the issue, as she had thought she was untouchable. Bad mistake to make when your immediate boss does not like being told "If you touch me, my VIP boyfriend will sack you".

Ken sacked Jackie. To be honest, I felt sorry for her as Ken sacked her. I was watching Diane's face; she had been sneering when they came in, but now she was smirking. I knew that as Jackie was now without a wage packet, Diane would throw her out of the bedsit. Not a nice position to be in: homeless and pregnant.

The next day when Diane came into work, and as tensions between us had eased, she was toeing the line and was fully aware of my new position. We sat talking, and Diane told me Jackie was no longer living at the bedsit with her. Diane had told her to leave the night before when she had gotten home from her shift. No surprise there; we had known that would be Diane's next move. Let's face it, you were only ever a friend to Diane when you had money or a use.

While all of this had been going on, Robert and I were still seeing each other; however, Ken had started getting even more flirty than he had been before. Since Vera's leaving, there had been no obvious Vera replacement, and Slimy and his girlfriend Joleen were becoming, it seemed, more and more serious about each other.

As was the way of managers in the pub trade of the day, they all seemed as if their todgers had a life of their own, not content with just the one woman they were seeing: Ken and his harem, Slimy with his Joleen, who when she was not on shift, his todger was poking about in any bit of skirt that showed an interest, and Richard with the barmaids. At the end of most shifts, Slimy would be out the door with a different woman every time; Richard kept his amours in-house, being a bit more select.

Then came the Christmas dinner. I was going to my mother's house for lunch; my dad was picking me up. I was due back in work that night. We were having roast goose that Christmas, not my favourite giblet stew with dumplings, but my mother made giblet gravy, so not so bad. Richard had asked if I would bring him a portion back, saying it had been years since he had tasted goose. After the Christmas dinner shift at work, the staff were being given a Christmas meal before the night shift started. Back in the seventies, most Trophy Inns still opened for Christmas Day, but bookings only. To be fair, it would have been stupid not to open, as they made a killing in trade.

Upon my arrival back at work that Christmas night, Joleen was standing on top of the bar in the upstairs restaurant, replacing the holly that had somehow fallen down, along with some of the Christmas baubles which were intertwined with the holly. Joleen was singing a kind of ditty about how it was all pricks and balls this Christmas, which I took to mean the decorations she was sorting out, until I saw the door to the upstairs landlord's flat where Ken and Beryl lived open, and out came one of the upstairs barmaids. At first, I did not twig what had been going on until Joleen made a point of pointing at this girl, singing away about pricks and balls this Christmas, continuing to point at the barmaid who was blushing really badly.

Beryl was not at the pub, having gone to family for the day. As the barmaid came further down the stairs, she was followed by Ken, who was hastily rearranging his clothes. It seems the barmaid had been Ken's Christmas gift. Nothing to do with me what he got up to, but it did make my life a bit harder that night as this silly barmaid took it to mean that as Ken had shagged her, she was now able to do whatever she wanted, except work.

I really was not impressed. I had to go to Ken to try and talk to him about the situation, which was hard as he was quite tipsy – unusual for him, but then it was Christmas.

I asked Ken if I could see him in the office. Big mistake; but as I've said before, at that point, I was quite naive.

In the office, I started to try and explain to Ken that, by his actions, this barmaid, who was a newbie, thought she could now toss it off at work, which not only affected me but all the other staff having to pick up her slack. Ken came across the office, which was really tiny, grabbing me while I was talking, kissing me, and running his hands all over my body. As I struggled, he put his hands down my top, pinching my nipples. I managed to shove him away, slapping his face furiously. The slap startled him, sobering him up somewhat. He apologised, saying that he had fancied me since I began at the Arms, so it seemed the flirting he had been doing was meant after all. In my naivety, I had not realized he had meant it. I left the office very shaken and worried as obviously Ken, being my boss, may now have taken umbrage at my repulsing his advances.

Richard came around the corner as I left, looking at me; he knew there was something wrong. He took my arm, asking me what was wrong. I explained. Richard assured me Ken would not be nasty to me going forward, saying he's pissed; he won't remember, which is a good thing. As far as you're concerned, just don't put yourself in that position again. It's unusual for Ken, as we all know, when at work he behaves himself; it's do as I say, not do as I do. It's because he's drunk, he's acted like this.

Do not forget this was the early seventies, long before all the equality at work and different types of workplace protocols came into being. In the seventies, to be honest, we were not very far from the deeds and actions that took place in the Middle Ages, where an employer would use his workforce as he saw fit in whatever manner he chose, be it getting the maid pregnant and then casting her off to fend for herself or any kind of harassment. To take an employer to tribunal just was not heard of.

Robert came to pick me up that night. I was still a bit unsettled. He asked me what was wrong. I just said it had been a bad day at work; no good telling him for one, not a lot he could do, and I did not want to get in the way of his friendship with Ken.

The next day, although I was quite wary going into work, Ken was quite normal. Nothing more was said about the day before apart from Ken having the mightiest hangover going, served him right. Ken was talking to me about various things to do with the pub when he started slagging Richard off as usual, calling him "Jew boy" and "no balls prick". I flipped, telling Ken he was out of order; that Richard, considering what was going on in his personal life, was a standup guy. Ken was taken aback, but to my surprise, never said another word about Richard in my presence.

We then went on to discuss rotas, Ken telling me Slimy was not well and would not be in work for a couple of days. I asked what the problem was; Ken said he's caught a dose!

Again, my naivety, I asked what's a dose. Ken looked at me, saying, "Are you joking? You know, a dose – venereal disease. Yuk!"

A couple of days later, Slimy came back into work. Unusually for Slimy, he started talking to me; usually he spoke to me like shit. To be fair, he spoke to everyone like shit, except Ken. I asked him if he felt better. He replied, "A bit, but that's to be expected when you have a dose." I was shocked; I had not expected him to tell me that. Such things were extremely personal and not to be discussed.

I said, "Well, I hope Joleen is well, as I have heard VD is very transmissible." Slimy laughed, saying, "Joleen does not care. Any other girl would, but not Joleen – she won't give up on sex just because I have a dose." My reply was, "So who's given it to who? As obviously you two are in a relationship, so which one has been playing away and brought VD back?"

Slimy never confirmed which one of the pair was at fault; he just turned on his heel and walked away, obviously realising he had said too much.

That night, Ken was not at the pub, which was unusual. Richard had left me to run the upstairs, only coming up near the end of business. We sat chatting, watching the staff work. Richard was saying Ken had been called out early that morning by the police; Richard did not know if it was a problem with one of Ken's other pubs.

A customer came through the doors asking if he could get a meal as it was past last orders. Richard said no, but you may get one downstairs if they are still busy. The customer went off, and Richard and I continued to chat, laughing about some things. As we did, the doors flew open with a crash as Slimy cannoned through them. I was startled. He charged over to us, ranting about Richard sending the customer downstairs to try and obtain a meal. Richard told him to calm down. At that point, he jumped at me, saying, "You were laughing at me about it."

Me, stunned much!

I told Slimy, "Yes, Richard and I were laughing, but not at you." Slimy was having none of it. The little prick was incandescent with rage, telling me, "Right, you, in the office."

Again, stunned much! I pointed at my chest, saying, "Who, me? In the office for what? And who the bloody hell do you think you're talking to, you jumped-up little prick?"

At that point, he stepped back, realising what an absolute twat he was being – not just in front of us but the whole upstairs floor. What a knob! But also, that I had faced him off; he really had not expected that.

He went off back downstairs, ranting about telling Ken what had happened when Ken was next in. Richard and I just looked at each other, stunned.

The next time I saw Ken was a few days later, as our shifts had not connected. Ken mentioned the Slimy fracas, asking me what happened, to which I gave my explanation. Ken said, "Fine, don't worry about it."

I replied, "I'm not. I did nothing wrong." Which I think surprised Ken, but by this point, I was learning to stand up for myself.

Robert was supposed to be in that night to see me, but very unusually did not turn up. The next night was Ken's usual group night when his friends would come in, and he would have a meal with them all. Robert and his wife were not there, but his friend Derick was. Derick waited until Ken left the bar, beckoning me over and asking me if I had heard about Robert and Ken falling out.

I was stunned, saying no. Derick proceeded to explain that, as I've said previously, they all drove Jaguar cars, Robert being in a top position within Jaguar. Apparently, some discrepancies within Robert's department had led to a fraud crime investigation within that department. Robert was under suspicion and had to supply the police with all sorts of information for their investigation, at which point Ken's name had come up.

Ken was not averse to obtaining free services if he could from anybody, hence the hull-age book for police freebies, as I have mentioned earlier.

Derick said both the police had interviewed Ken and Robert. Robert had been told in no uncertain terms by Ken never to show his face at the pub again.

Now, I know for a fact Ken had been given services at Jaguar by Robert for free. What I did not know was that among all the fraud inquiries, an amount of high-end sweeteners had disappeared also. Back in those days, Jaguar was the be-all and end-all of the car to have. Like the goody bags film stars are given these days when attending film premieres, these goody bags were given out to high rollers who were either having Jaguars fitted out to their own specs or had already had Jaguars delivered. This was Jaguar's way of retaining and promoting their cars through existing customers or getting those customers to pull their friends and acquaintances in to purchase Jaguar cars – very high-priced goods; Rolex watches, to name one high-end brand, were contained in those bags. I will always remember Robert coming into the pub one night wearing one of the first-ever digital watches on the market at that time, at a cost of some three hundred pounds, which these days you can pick up for a couple of quid. Ken was adamant he had taken none of them. Robert apparently was getting the blame for the goody bags, as they were under lock and key in his department.

Derick told me Robert would ring you soon on the downstairs phone, which was in a private cubicle so no one could hear our conversation.

Robert knew Ken would be out at a certain time the next day, so my phone call was arranged for then.

The next day, my duly arranged call came through. Robert was heartbroken, saying he had trusted Ken. Yes, he had given Ken some free services, but the missing goody bags – very expensive bags – were none of his doing. The only people with access to where the bags had been kept were Robert and, on a couple of occasions, Robert had left Ken in the bag store on his own while Robert saw to Ken's Jaguar. Ken was the only other person who had access to them. Now, as we all knew, Ken was devious, especially in his dealings with the police. All coppers knew that if you were after a freebie, The Arms was the place to go – you scratched their back, they scratched yours. Robert was adamant Ken was the culprit. Poor fool, Robert thought Ken was a trusted friend.

Robert said, "I am not going to be able to see you for a while", as not only did I work at The Arms, but I lived in as well, in the adjoining staff quarters. Sandra, Robert's wife, was justifiably upset over the situation and was keeping Robert on a tight lead – a very upsetting situation all around. Robert was suspended from work, and a criminal trial was looming, as Ken had said he could prove everything he had done at Jaguar. He had paid for it; he had the receipts to prove it. Of course he did; Robert had issued receipts for work Ken had paid for, but as anyone knows, you can get a receipt for one thing while at the same time obtaining far more than what's listed on the receipt.

Robert had been daft enough to then give Ken free services; of course, Ken wouldn't have a receipt for those. At the same time, no one had any proof of anything that had gone missing from the Bags store, and Robert, even though he had admitted giving free services – a big cost to a Jaguar in those days – had effectively sealed his own fate. If you're giving free services, what else might you be giving away or taking that you should not have?

To say I was in turmoil was an understatement, so God knows what Robert and his wife felt like. Now I was going to have to continue working alongside Ken, whom I knew was corrupt, but this had sunk to a whole new level.

Ken was his usual self, as if nothing had happened. In fact, he was quite chirpy. As the days wore on, it became apparent Ken was cocksure of himself about the looming court case. Ken knew I was upset over it all, as Robert and I had been seeing each other by this time for well over eighteen months, and Ken's flirtatious attitude towards me was becoming more intense – almost as if he were rubbing my nose in the fact I could not see Robert anymore.

It was almost like a tribal chieftain selecting a new partner from his harem, of which we all knew Ken had women situated in all the pubs in his area. As the days wore on, my ex-husband turned up at the pub now and then, trying to talk to me, which I really did not want to engage in; as far as I was concerned, that phase of my life was over. Richard spoke to him, telling him he would have to leave the pub as he was making a pest of himself. My ex had brought a handbag to the pub that I had left at his flat as an excuse to try and speak to me, which he threw at Richard. At that point, Richard escorted my ex from the pub. I was very upset, not only because I had not wanted my ex anywhere near me, but also by the scenes he was causing at my place of work. Richard said, "Don't worry, he's been told in no uncertain terms not to come back." This scene, plus the Robert and Ken situation, had left my emotional state very fragile, which may go some way to explain why that night I found myself alone after shift in Ken's company. Richard had gone to another of Ken's pubs on an errand. It was unusually quiet that night, so downstairs had finished and gone. It was the first time ever I had found myself alone with Ken, and to be truthful, I was not thinking straight.

Ken asked me if I would like a drink as we cashed up, which I accepted, not thinking. Ken was chatting away; before I knew it, we were on our second drink. I really don't know at what point I started crying, and he put his arm around my shoulder. The next thing I knew, Ken had me crushed up against the bar, kissing me. I struggled to get away; the next thing I was on the floor with Ken on top of me, his hands up my skirt, pulling at my pants, which tore as he forced his cock inside me. When it was over, he withdrew, adjusting his clothes, rising from the floor where he had left me like a used dishcloth. At the same time, he told me he had always wanted to fuck me, that as I lived in staff accommodation to which he had passkeys, he would be visiting me whenever he felt like it, and I would do whatever he asked of me, as Robert would not be coming back and was in no position to help me.

I was terrified, distraught, shaking like a jelly. Ken just walked away towards the gents' loo. I stumbled up, running downstairs, letting myself out and into my room at the staff quarters. Luckily for me, on my door was a bolt as well as the door lock, which I fastened. I sat sobbing, knowing I was now in a really bad situation. My mother had always told me since leaving home not to try and come back; her phrase was, "You have made your bed; you lie in it." Robert could not help; my ex-husband would not help, even if I had asked him to. It was no good going to the police; Ken had them all in his back pocket. Besides the fact that back in those days, if you had a few boyfriends, you were known as a good-time girl or asking for it.

I sat in that room all night, going over and over what had happened and trying to fathom out what to do. The next morning, luckily for me, Ken would not be in work; he had to go to one of his other pubs, giving me time to calm myself and appear normal as I worked. Richard was not having any of it; he was a very intuitive man. I saw him watching me a couple of times as I worked. He came over to me, saying, "Chris, can you help me in the office for a few minutes?" In the office, he said, "Right, what's wrong?" I said nothing. He just looked at me, saying, "No, something is really off with you today. I got back here last night to find Ken sitting in the upstairs bar quite drunk and nobody about. I came looking for you, but your room light was out. It was really early; I know you were in there. Come on, spill." I just burst into tears again, sobbing uncontrollably.

Richard calmed me down; he couldn't have been nicer or more supportive, which made it all the worse in my mind. Falteringly, I told Richard what had happened.

Richard blamed himself, saying, "I told you never to be on your own with Ken." He also said "if it hadn't been for your ex causing trouble yesterday and you not thinking straight, you would not have let yourself be put in that situation". But he also agreed it was a waste of time going to the police.

Richard promised me under no circumstances would I ever be on my own with Ken ever again.

IT'S ALL PRICKS AND BALLS THIS CHRISTMAS, & GIBLET STEW

He told me he had a friend who ran a hotel in Kidderminster. If I wanted to, he would arrange a meeting with his friend to see if I could get a job at his friend's hotel. He would cover for me with Ken, telling Ken I had to have a couple of days' holiday to sort out my ex-issues.

Ken could like it or lump it.

The next day, Richard came to my room, telling me his friend had agreed to give me an interview. I was to go over to Kidderminster by train that day, where his friend would pick me up from the station.

At the station, Richard's friend picked me up. He had his small daughter in the car with him. His friend Roy introduced himself and his daughter, Daniella. We started off to the hotel. Roy was chatting away to me; his daughter was about four years old. Roy was telling me his wife, Susan, and himself had had the hotel for about two years, but it wasn't doing very well at the moment. It did need a bit of refurbishment, and because of that, the local college was hiring rooms from Roy to house Iranian students. Kidderminster had a shortage of student accommodation. These Iranian students had been given camp beds, just like the Army had used in the Second World War – a bit of canvas over a metal frame, which had been placed in the corridors of the college. Not ideal by any standards, so they had approached Roy to help out with accommodation.

Roy had jumped at the chance of a bit of incoming revenue. As we chatted, Daniella asked her dad for some sweets. Roy told her, "When we get back to the hotel." Daniella replied, "Dad, you said if I came with you in the car, I could get some sweets." Roy said, "No, Daniella, you must wait until we get home." At that, Daniella let out such a scream, throwing herself back and forth in the car like a demented demon. Oh my God!

Roy just carried on driving, totally ignoring his demented child. This was before the days of compulsory seat belt use in cars or child safety seats.

Once we arrived at the hotel, Roy got out of the car; Daniella was still screaming and banging about in the back. Roy just walked away, leaving her to it. I said, "What about your daughter?" Roy said, "My wife will come out and get her." As we entered the front door, a woman was coming towards us. Roy introduced her as his wife, Susan. Roy said, "Daniella is still in the car; you had better go get her."

Roy asked me if I would like a cup of tea, showing me into the bar area, then going off to obtain the tea. A few minutes later, Susan and Daniella came in.

Susan gave Daniella some toys to play with, settling the now quiet child in a corner, by which time Roy had come back with tea for the three of us.

Roy and Susan explained they rented the hotel from a businessman. Previously, they had been in the pub trade in Wales, where they had made quite a bit of money – so much so that for a period of time, they had actually bought a boat, which they had sailed around the world on. Daniella had been born during this hiatus, so she had enjoyed the unparalleled focus of both parents. They admitted she was spoiled rotten, hence the tantrums if she did not get her own way. They had an older child, Becky, who was at school and whom I was to meet at a later period.

Roy said the hotel had some events booked in that were soon to be upcoming and would need additional help, as Richard had told Roy about my previous managerial experience with Crown Wallpapers and the fact that I was now a fully trained pub under manager across all aspects of that trade. He was quite anxious for me to start at the hotel, saying I would be an asset. Considering the predicament I was in at the Arms, I agreed to start the next week. To be honest, if I could have started that day, I would have, as there was no way I wanted to go back to the Arms and face Ken, but I knew Richard had my back, so it was all arranged.

When I got back to the Arms later that afternoon, Richard was waiting for me, asking how it had gone. I filled him in, saying my only concern was having to work around Ken and his threat of getting into my room whenever he liked. Richard said, "Don't worry, Ken is going to be occupied elsewhere." I was puzzled, asking Richard what he meant. He said, "You will see later."

That night, I went on shift to find Diane standing in Ken's corner with him, having drinks. Diane was not working that night; I steered clear of Ken's corner while I worked, only going to it when I needed something to do with the shift. Ken was making it very obvious Diane had become the new member of his harem at the Arms. Fine by me; it kept his focus off me. Diane was lapping up the attention; she was well aware of the perks that came with harem membership, in addition to the fact she thought she had got one over on me by being his new harem member. At one point, as I stood chatting to a customer near Ken's corner, Diane made a snide comment along the lines of "Shouldn't your floor manageress be working and not fraternising with customers while other customers are waiting to be seated?"; Ken just smirked at that comment while staring straight at me.

At the end of the shift, after cashing up, Ken and Diane were acting like two naughty schoolkids, taking soda siphons from the bar, chasing each other around and squirting soda water at each other, which, considering Ken's stance on professionalism at work, really made him look a bit sad, as all the staff were watching these antics while waiting for staff taxis, with various expressions on their faces: bemusement, scorn, amazement. Ken had always preached the "keep your private life away from your work life" ethic, except for the fact that every single person, be it staff or customers, knew Ken couldn't keep his todger in his trousers; some customers, as I have said, openly calling him Lecherous Ken.

This type of behaviour was so out of character. As staff taxis started to arrive to pick up the waiting staff, Richard came up to our floor to support me. Along with Richard came a young manager who ran one of Ken's pubs in Kenilworth. Diane was straight on him like a rash. Ken didn't seem that bothered but was watching me as he spoke to his young manager. The fact that this manager had turned up made my situation slightly easier, or so I thought, as Ken really couldn't make a scene with him being there.

The last member of staff left, leaving Ken, Diane, myself, Richard, and this young manager in our bar. I went to the shelf behind the bar where my handbag was, and taking out my written notice, with Richard by my side, I walked up to Ken, handing my notice to him, saying, "This is my notice. I am leaving at the end of the week. I have holidays untaken, which I will use to enable me to leave within the period of notice I've given you."

Ken was furious, telling me he wanted to see me in the office immediately. I replied, "Fine, if Richard accompanies us." Diane strutted over, asking what was going on – not that it was any of her business – but I told her I had just given notice. Diane was shocked; I think she thought, as Ken's latest harem member, she would be able to lord it over me. Even though she had apologised to me in the past for her behaviour, it had really gone against the grain for her to have to apologise, which she had done to enable her to keep her job – the job which was a cover for her main job as an escort – in a pivotal position for her main pick-up trade at the Arms.

The young manager came across, speaking to Diane, allowing Richard, Ken, and me to go into the office. Once there, Ken turned on Richard, telling him to leave. Richard said, "No way am I leaving Chris on her own with you. I know what happened," which gave Ken a bit of a start. Richard proceeded to tell Ken he knew what Ken called him behind his back: "Jew boy and no balls prick" etc. Richard said, "You can call me all the names you like, but at least I'm not the type of man you are, who forces himself on a vulnerable young woman."

Ken was incandescent with rage that Richard was standing up to him. Like I had said all along, people called Richard names because of the situation he was in with his wife. However, I knew Richard was far from a coward. No man worth his salt would put up with that sort of treatment unless he had a backbone made of steel, which, by standing up to Ken for me, was becoming blatantly obvious to Ken. At that moment, the office door banged open as Diane strutted in. The cheek of her still amazes me to this day. She demanded to know what was going on, saying, "Have you told her–" meaning me– "that you and I are in a relationship, Ken, and she needs to speak to me with respect." I turned on Diane, saying, "I have always treated every member of staff here with respect, including you, despite all that's gone on. Whatever you are doing with Ken is nothing to do with me, especially now that I am leaving. I was going to work until the end of the week; however, now I'm out of here. You're welcome to the letch. I hope you have better luck than all those who have gone before you."

At that, I opened the door, walking through it with Richard behind me. Richard accompanied me back to the staff rooms, telling me, "Don't worry about anything tonight. You have locks on your door, but because Ken will be occupied with Diane, he won't have the time or energy to try and bother you, and I will be listening out."

I went to bed having a fitful sleep, waking at every little sound. The next morning, I packed my stuff, ringing my Dad from the phone box just outside the Arms, asking Dad if I could stay at home for two nights until I started my new job. Dad was all for it, telling me, "Don't worry about your mother; I will tell her you're staying." I don't know what Dad said to my mother, but she never said a word apart from asking me what the new job was and where.

CHAPTER 8

On the day I was due to start at the Park Attwood, Dad drove me over to Kidderminster, telling me, "If ever you need to come home, don't hesitate." I told Dad, "Mum won't like that; she told me never to come back home." Dad said, "You're my daughter; if you want to visit, you're welcome." My dad never ever stood up to my mum, so this was quite a big thing for him to do.

I was quite worried about Richard and any repercussions from Ken. Richard had told me to phone him once I was settled at the Park Attwood. To me, Richard was like the big brother I never had.

Arriving at the Park Attwood, I was thrown in at the deep end. Once Dad had gone and I had unpacked, Roy, the owner, called me into the office, outlining the events coming up and what he exactly wanted me to do. It started that night with several reservations for the restaurant. Roy was the chef, and Sue, his wife, was the hostess. My role was kind of barmaid, waitress, and hostess, depending on what Sue and Roy needed.

That night, as I took orders from people using the restaurant, I had to go through a glass conservatory to the kitchen to place the orders with Roy. The first time I walked into that kitchen, I was appalled. What a shithole! My God, if health and safety or food standards had ever walked in, they would have closed it down on the spot. Bearing in mind this was the mid-seventies, where these types of agencies were not as hot on hygiene as they are these days, the kitchen table was piled high with dirty dishes, most still containing their original foodstuffs in various stages of decomposition. Dirty ashtrays, dirty linens – you name it, all thrown in a big rotting pile. The smell was awful. There was a big range along one wall where Roy stood cooking – no whites, just his normal attire. Along the far wall was a big industrial dishwashing machine, which I don't think had been used for months, as it still contained rancid water. Wherever you looked was filth. I think Roy and Sue had a sense of complacency about it all.

As the Park Attwood was way out in the countryside, with no buses or any form of transport to take me away – even if I had somewhere to go – I had to basically get on with it. After the last customer had gone, I went straight to Roy and Sue, informing them how appalled I was and why. They both admitted they had let things get out of hand, telling me I could do whatever I wanted to put things to rights.

The next morning, I got the odd job man they had there, Joe, to help me clean up the shithole that was the kitchen. The next step was a full overhaul of the bar and ballroom. By the time we had finished, everywhere was gleaming. I went up to change for that night's trade.

As I came downstairs for that shift, a couple of blokes were talking to Roy and Sue in the foyer. Roy called me over, introducing me to them. One was an architect; the other, a very distinguished-looking bloke who was the owner of vast swathes of land both here and abroad, with various companies dealing in all sorts of trades. The two men were not just friends but also business partners, both as rich as Midas. The more distinguished one, Graham, had driven them both to the hotel that night in his gold Rolls-Royce. The other one, Nigel, was laughing, saying it's our boys' night out.

I excused myself, saying I had to get on with prep for that night's trade. Sue followed me into the kitchen, and as we got out of earshot of Graham and Nigel, Sue told me never to let myself get caught alone with Nigel; he's a real letch. Bloody hell, had I really jumped out of the frying pan into the fire here or what? Sue went on to say the hotel was having financial difficulties, as trade was not as good as they were led to believe when they had taken it on. Graham and particularly Nigel had been a great help in keeping them afloat; at one point, Nigel had taken Sue to the local wholesalers to buy a full inventory for the bar when, due to the hotel not paying bills with the wholesalers, they had stopped deliveries.

However, after the wholesalers' trip, Nigel had booked a room overnight, being a bit too tipsy to drive. When Sue had taken Nigel some towels up to the room, he had been stark naked, saying payment was due for the bar inventory he had just purchased. As it happened, Roy had come along a few seconds later, calling her name, which had startled Nigel, giving Sue the chance to escape. Or so she said, considering the fact that both these men, Nigel in particular, were basically still keeping the Attwood afloat in various ways, and Nigel was very smarmy around Sue at all times. I had my own opinion as to whether that debt had been paid in kind and was still being used as a bartering tool for ongoing funds donated to the Attwood. Sue said she had not told Roy about the incident, as obviously, Nigel was keeping them afloat at that point for one. Secondly, she had not wanted any altercation between Roy and Nigel, and the following morning, Nigel had not mentioned the event. Sue did not know if Nigel had been so drunk he could not remember or if he was using that fact as an excuse not to mention it in any way. However, Sue would never put herself in that position again, and obviously, if there came a time when Nigel's help was needed again, it was wiser to pretend that event had never happened – a catch-22 situation on behalf of both Sue and Nigel. From the way Sue and Nigel were together, I firmly believed that bartering, shall we call it, was ongoing between Nigel and Sue with the full knowledge of Roy.

I asked Sue if the other chap, Graham, was as bad. Sue said no; she had only good things to say about Graham, that he was a really nice chap.

Sue and I carried on into the kitchen, which that morning had been gleaming with cleanliness. On the kitchen table was a great big pile of dirty dishes, among which were soggy, stubbed-out cigarette ends, which turned my stomach. I do not smoke, finding it a very dirty habit. I turned to Sue, demanding to know where all these dishes had come from, bearing in mind my hard work to clean what had been a shit hole. Sue confessed they were from her and Roy's private rooms. I told her it was disgusting to put cigarettes out on food plates. She said she couldn't be bothered to get an ashtray. I told her in no uncertain terms I did not appreciate her doing that after all my hard graft, telling her, "You did it, so you clean it." Sue went to put the dishes in the sink. I stopped her, saying, "No, in the dishwasher, please." Sue said we don't use the dishwasher; it costs too much to run. My reply was, "It's been cleaned out; you will use it as it runs at high temperature, allowing better hygiene. You have not been using it because you have not been cleaning anything. That stops now. Before the end of any shift going forward, the kitchen will be left spotless."

Sue was very taken aback, but to hell with it; if I were staying there, it would run to proper standards.

That evening, trade was really slow, so after a while, I was able to go into the bar where Graham started chatting to me, asking me about myself. Graham started telling me all about the shoot that used the hotel in season. As it happened, that coming weekend a shoot was due to take place. I had never liked blood sports and still don't, but it was the hotel's business and quite lucrative. Graham asked me if I had ever had pheasant. I replied no, so he said he would give me a brace from the shoot that weekend, asking me if I could cook, as the shoot usually had lunch and tea at the hotel. Considering how rich they all were and the high-class menus they usually had in their lives, at shoot lunches they requested bangers and mash for lunch and crumpets for tea, which I found quite funny. Graham went on to say the usual gravy served with the bangers and mash was really horrible; could I improve on it? My reply was, "Let's put it this way: Is the Pope Catholic?" which really amused Graham.

On shoot days, the beaters they used to flush pheasants out were young offenders from a local detention centre who had earned the privilege of a day out of jail, a good lunch, and a pint of lager, but only one pint. These lads were fed on the lower floor of the hotel, accompanied by guards, while the shoot gentry enjoyed their lunch on the mid terrace.

That first day, as the shoot lined up helping themselves to food, I stood at the end of the buffet serving out my homemade gravy. Graham was my first customer. He said, "No gravy for me." I said, "Oh, go on, try a little bit; it's homemade by me." He took a tiny bit from my ladle with the tip of his knife. The smile he gave was beaming as he said, "Wow! Guys, you all have to try this gravy; Chris made it, it's awesome!" Then he turned back to me, saying, "A full ladle, please."

One after another, all the shoot had gravy, complimenting me on it. Sue was not as impressed; previously Sue had made the gravy, which, to be honest, was disgusting as she recycled leftover soups, which she said was how all the kitchens she had ever worked in had made gravy. Remind me never to have high-class gravy anywhere, as it's all recycled crap at a very expensive cost, whereas my gravy was quite simply made from the juices and fat leftover from the bangers the shoot were having with their mash and veg, and the caramelised onions I had put out for them, thickened with flour and good old-fashioned gravy browning, then the juices of the vegetables served up to them.

That day, the shoot was very happy with their lunch. I was made up as one shooter after another praised my food and my gravy. Once the shoot was served, I then took the beaters their lunch – not a hot lunch for them but substantial, big, thick-cut sandwiches and chunks of cheese and pork pies, real hearty food, served with big jugs of chilled frothy lager. Those lads really enjoyed their lunch while enjoying freedom for a few hours.

All very polite to me; it's not my business why they had found themselves in jail. There but for the grace of God go I.

After lunch, the shoot all went back out to murder some more birds while I cleaned up lunch debris, then started preparing huge pots of tea and plates of crumpets for their return. It always amazed me that they enjoyed those crumpets so much, considering their wealth and status in life. They could have been dining on steak and caviar; they were kind of like little schoolboys wagging a day off school.

At the back of the hotel stood a big Chuckie Chicken farm run by an ex-soldier, Matt. He would come into the hotel at night for a drink – sometimes on his own, sometimes with his wife. Not a bad chap; we chatted often. I had told him about Graham offering me the pheasants. He seemed a bit taken aback at that offer, telling me Graham must really like me. "Do you know how much these gents pay for that day's shooting? That brace of pheasants will easily have cost Graham about two hundred pounds." I was really shocked, having not given any thought to costs; two hundred pounds was a real wedge back then. I told him when I got them, he could have one – two would be way too much for me. He was dead pleased, saying, "It's been years since we had pheasant. If you give me both of them, my wife will dress yours for you" – saved me getting messy. He told me how the Chuckie Chicken farm was run, how every twelve weeks the lorry turns up at the site to process the chickens right on the spot and straight into the lorry – kind of like factory ships at sea. He also told me tales of how rats preyed on the chickens at the site, so at night he would climb into the rafters of the site, shooting rats as they appeared. Back then, Chuckie Chicken was a well-known name. If consumers saw the sight I saw when they were processed and smelled the smell of that site, no one would have ever bought Chuckie Chicken. Maybe that's why they are no longer heard of in the UK. Matt then trotted back off to his work, leaving me to mine, telling me he would pop over later for the pheasants.

The shooters duly turned up for their tea, filled themselves with tea and crumpets. Graham came over to me, giving me a brace of birds but telling me to keep it quiet that he had given them to me. Obviously, such was the cost of them; I suppose he didn't want the others to see he was favouring me. I thanked him, and off he went. A few days later, Graham and Nigel turned back up at the hotel for their usual drinking session. Nigel wandered off, chatting to Roy and Sue, leaving Graham in the bar with me. Graham asked me if I had a boyfriend. I said no. He then proceeded to tell me he had a mistress of several years, but recently, as these things go, the relationship had come to an end – his words. The next morning, he was flying to Bermuda on his private aeroplane. Would I like to go with him and become his mistress?

I'm still trying to pick my jaw up off the floor all these years later over that one. I told him, "No, thank you, Graham. I have just gotten out of a bad marriage and a particularly bad job where the boss had assaulted me," not telling him I had actually been raped. "You seem a really nice guy, but I am not in a place where I want another relationship at the moment."

Graham told me to think it over and that he would send his chauffeur to me the next morning to see if I had changed my mind. Even if I had, I did not possess a passport, so I couldn't have gone anyway. Thinking Graham was his usual tipsy self, I presumed it was all harmless, that what he was saying would be forgotten by the time his head hit the pillow that night.

Shortly after that conversation, Graham and Nigel went home. I never gave it another thought, except that Graham had been quite tipsy.

Until the next morning when Roy came banging on my bedroom door, telling me there's someone to see you downstairs, who turned out to be Graham's chauffeur.

The chauffeur told me the boss sent him to pick me up. I politely told the chauffeur to tell Graham no thank you. I did tell him last night I would not be taking him up on his offer. The chauffeur smiled, saying, "You do realise he won't be back for some months and usually gets what he wants." Again, I repeated my no thank you, at which point the chauffeur left.

To this day, I still can't believe I had that offer, and I often wonder how my life would have turned out if I had taken Graham up on his offer. It's very reminiscent of the George Michael song "Turn a Different Corner".

Still, I will never know, as by the time Graham was due back, I had left The Park Attwood and Kidderminster, coming back to Coventry.

At the Park Attwood at that time, among the Iranian students living there, were a few who spoke reasonable English. One, Sher, was the son of a diplomat; he drove a TR7, which was the car to be seen in those days. Sher had unlimited money. His girlfriend was English. Another, Ahmad, was the son of a doctor, also with an English girlfriend. Ahmad's girlfriend, Maggie, actually lived with him in his room at the hotel, while Sher's girlfriend was brought to the hotel by Sher for short periods of time. Then there was Mustapha, a really nice chap I nicknamed Mushy, which he did not mind, and Behrooz, who was really attractive and seemed really nice, offering to help me around the hotel with heavy jobs.

All of these Iranian chaps, except maybe Ahmad and Maggie, who had become engaged, made it blatantly obvious that their girlfriends were only girlfriends for the duration of their stay in the UK.

After Amhad and Maggie got engaged, Sher's girlfriend made it blatantly obvious she wanted more from Sher. Behrooz and I had become very friendly; he would tell me lots of stuff about the others, their goings-on, and relationships. Behrooz said Sher would never get engaged to his girlfriend, as he was already promised by his dad to another high-profile diplomat's daughter back in Iran, and that Sher was only using his girlfriend for sex while in the UK. I felt really sorry for that girl; she had never spoken to me, but from what I observed, she seemed really nice. One day, shortly after Amhad and Maggie got engaged, Sher's girl came downstairs from his room in floods of tears, asking me to call her a taxi. Before I could ask her, what was wrong, Sher came charging down the stairs, grabbing his girl by the arm and escorting her to his car. He sat her in the passenger seat and drove away.

The next day, Sher and his girl came back; his girl was wearing a ring on her engagement finger. Nothing to do with me, but I felt so happy for her; it seemed she had gotten what she wanted. That was until Behrooz and I were talking later that day, and he told me Sher had said to the lads it's a friendship ring bought to keep his girl quiet, but his girl thinks it's an engagement ring.

Dastardly, but none of my business. The poor girl now thought she was engaged when, in actual fact, she was being used.

I should have known then, but like I said, I was very naive at that point, so I did not pick up on certain signals and situations.

By this time, Behrooz had asked me out on a date, which I accepted. Roy and Sue did not like that, but it was my life; as long as it did not affect my work, it was none of their business, so I accepted.

Behrooz seemed so kind, caring, and helpful. We went out on quite a few dates around my work hours – meals out, trips into town, the usual boy-and-girl stuff. This went on for several months, during which I learned Behrooz had a large family in Tehran, the capital of Iran. He had done his national service prior to coming to the UK, and his dad, Nassar, was a general in the Iranian Army. His family was quite wealthy, owning shops in the bazaars, farms, and property in Tehran.

This was in the time of the Shah, before his overthrow some years later when the Ayatollah Khomeini, a religious nutcase, seized power from the Shah.

One night, Behrooz took me for an Indian meal at a really nice restaurant in Kidderminster. The table was candlelit. Behrooz ordered champagne, something I had never had before, and to be honest, although I never said anything to him after tasting it, I could not see what all the fuss was about.

At the end of the meal, Behrooz was telling me he would never go back to Iran. When I asked him why not, he said, "Because I want you to marry me, and I want to spend the rest of my life here with you."

Come to think about it, years later, he had not said he loved me, but due to me being slightly tipsy at that point and the surprise at his proposal, I did not give the love word a thought. He told me he had been looking at engagement rings but thought I would like to choose one with him, which at the time I thought was a lovely thing to do.

God was I a naïve twit!

I accepted his proposal and went the next morning into town, where I chose an opal ring surrounded by rubies.

A few days later, while working alongside Roy and Sue in the hotel kitchen, I could see Sue gesturing to Roy, who asked her, "What's the matter? Are you having a fit?" It turned out Sue had spotted my engagement ring on my finger and was trying to tell Roy without me seeing her.

At that point, as they say, the jig was up, so I informed them both. Yes, Behrooz had asked me to marry him. They were both quite negative about my engagement, telling me I do realise these Iranian men only use girls here for sex. Just look at Sher and his girl. My reply was, yes, but look at Ahmad and Maggie – truly in love, engaged, and house hunting together. Although nothing more was said to me at that point, both Roy and Sue were unhappy I had flouted their rule and not only was dating a guest but had become engaged to that guest.

About a week later, there was a large wedding taking place at the hotel. Roy and Sue told me I would have to give up my room for the day to accommodate the bride, who would use my room to change into her going-away outfit. Unbeknownst to the bride, although she was paying for what she thought was a private room, it was, in actual fact, my room. So, I had to move all my belongings to the room of the Iranian couple, who had a room on the next floor up from me.

The Iranian husband was a lot older than his wife, who was pregnant, but he was the actual student retraining from his present job to become a doctor.

This couple was really nice; they were going to visit family that weekend, so would not be in their room.

Unbeknownst to me, Roy and Sue had not told this couple that in their absence, their room was going to be used by other people. On the day of the wedding, Roy came over to me, telling me not to go near the Iranian couple's room for at least two hours, as one of the wedding party had had a bit too much to drink. So, Roy told them they could have the room for a couple of hours for a lie down. Bang out of order, as not only was all my stuff in there, but all the Iranian couple's stuff as well.

It turned out to be more than a couple of hours, as the so-called tipsy person was, in actual fact, one of the bridesmaids bonking a guest. I witnessed their departure from the room sometime later as I was waiting to use the room to change for my evening shift duties. They were giggling and adjusting their attire as they left. As I entered the room, the bed was a mess, and there were used condoms in the wastebasket. As soon as I had changed, I confronted Roy, telling him what had happened and informing him that if he thought I was emptying that basket and changing that bed, he was wrong. I left it at that.

On Monday morning, the Iranian couple arrived back from their family visit, unaware of the use of their room over the weekend. A short while after their return, I was summoned to Roy and Sue's office, where the Iranian couple were sitting. Roy proceeded to tell me a very expensive pearl ring was missing from the couple's room and asked if I had anything to say about it, as the couple were going to call in the police if it was not found. In other words, Roy had told them I had used the room in their absence, but not all the other stuff that had gone on around their room that weekend.

I never even answered Roy; I just turned to the husband, who spoke quite good English, and fully informed him of everything that had happened in his room that weekend. I also told him, "If you will come with me to my room, you have my full permission to search my room yourself and all my belongings."

The husband stood up, saying, "No thank you, it's quite alright. I believe you," but I insisted I was not going to leave Roy and Sue with any wriggle room to come back at me at a later date. At that point, I knew my days at Park Attwood were over; not only were Roy and Sue devious, but they were also quite capable of blaming others for any problem they incurred upon themselves. All five of us traipsed along the landing to my room, where I insisted the husband search all my belongings. I even took my own jewellery box out, opening it up for Roy and the husband to search through.

Roy and Sue were looking very sheepish by the time my room had been tossed over, but I was determined that no blame of any sort could land at my door.

At the end of the search, the husband turned to Roy, telling him that as Roy had allowed their room, which had been paid for on a long-term lease, to be used without consulting him or his wife, the husband was holding Roy accountable for the ring, which he fully expected Roy to reimburse him for. If Roy did not, the husband would call in the police, as it was theft. He also told Roy in no uncertain terms that he found Roy's way of doing business disreputable at the least; therefore, he would not be renewing his term of lease with Roy.

He then turned to me, apologising that I had been put under suspicion of theft. After the husband and wife left my room, I flew at Roy and Sue, telling them exactly what I thought of them and giving my notice to leave, which was hard as I really had nowhere to go, or any other job lined up. But this had been the last straw; no way could I stay at the Park Attwood now.

I was due time off the day after this event happened, so I went into Kidderminster to look for work and other accommodation. Behrooz was obviously aware of the goings-on at the hotel and was really not happy about things there. As my fiancé, he stood by me, telling me if I was leaving, he was coming with me. Not to worry about accommodation; he had a friend in Kidderminster who rented out rooms – a lady named Lucy Price. Lucy owned two houses in Kidderminster. Behrooz took me along to visit Lucy, where we arranged to move into one of her vacant rooms the next week. Behrooz also told me not to worry about work at that point, as he would pay for things until I found another job – easier said than done in Kidderminster.

Behrooz and I went back to the Park Attwood so I could continue working out my notice and start gathering our belongings, ready to move to Lucy's house within the next few days.

Roy and Sue were not happy about my leaving, not so much because I was very good at my job and, in the period of time I had been at the hotel, had generated a lot of business – not only with the shoot guys and Graham and Nigel, but in my capacity as front of house by speaking to high-profile customers. All with connections in the area, the hotel's trade had increased tenfold just by my reputation as a person who knew her stuff, who could organise any event really well and not overcharge for these events. My personality, even though I say it myself, is pleasant, enabling me to communicate with the most difficult of customers in a very adept, businesslike manner while broadcasting a very approachable attitude, making some customers who think they are entitled to deference believe that that's what they are getting, when in actual fact they were deferring to me – doing and accepting what I needed them to accept.

Customers were actually contacting the hotel asking for me by name, saying this high-profile person or another had recommended the hotel to them by using my name, to ask for me when contacting the hotel for whatever event they needed to organise. In some ways, Roy and Sue would get a bit miffed about that; however, their business sense made them realise what an asset they had in me, so they deferred most of the running of the hotel to me.

Another reason Roy and Sue did not want us to leave was that Behrooz had told all his fellow students what had gone on with the wedding party and the missing ring, how Roy and Sue had tried to put the blame on me for the missing ring. The result of that was not only had the husband and wife given notice on their rental, but now the majority of the students had given notice also. As Behrooz said, if Roy and Sue can do that to Chris, who knows what's going on in the students' rooms when they are out of the hotel, and who will get the blame for missing items? In fact, one student had, as we thought, lost a solid gold Mohamed pendant given to him by his father. The student in question was sure he had the pendant in his room when he went out, but it was gone when he got back. There's always that element of doubt: Did I or did I not have it on me, or was it in my room? So, he had not raised too much fuss over the pendant's loss; now, however, he was questioning its loss.

The resulting exodus from the hotel was costing Roy and Sue thousands.

The night before we were due to leave, there was a big party of well-to-do customers booked in for a dinner. One of the gents asked for a particular port, which I knew Roy kept in the wine cellar. I went into the cellar to grab a bottle but could not reach the port. I'm quite small in height, so I rang up to Roy from the cellar intercom asking him to come down and assist me. Roy arrived in the cellar asking me which port I needed. I pointed up to the bottle on the rack above my head. Roy reached it down, and as I took the bottle from him and turned to walk away, he grabbed me from behind, thrusting himself up against me, pinning me between himself and the rack. I could feel his erection jabbing my buttocks as I struggled against him. The force of his movement shoved me against the racking so hard that the whole thing teetered forwards. A fortune in wine and port started to topple forward. Roy let me go, thrusting both his arms out to steady the rack. It was only the knee-jerk reaction and thought of all that money crashing to the floor that saved me. As he steadied the rack, he said, "You're dead lucky I nearly had you, but if you had thought about it for a second, you would have enjoyed it." My reply as I fled was, "Hell would freeze over first, and think yourself lucky I'm not telling Behrooz and the rest of the lads what you just tried."

I knew if I had told Behrooz there really would have been blood on the floor in that cellar. I high tailed it back up to the restaurant, depositing the port on the table of the customer, telling Sue, "That's it. I'm done. Serve them yourself. If you want to know why, ask Roy. Give me my severance pay now; I will say nothing more about what just happened between your husband and me in the wine cellar."

To my shock, Sue never uttered a word. She just took what money I was due from the till, not even making eye contact. I left the restaurant, going straight up to Behrooz in his room, telling him, "Sue has paid me; my shift is over. We are done here."

Behrooz was not stupid; he knew something had gone on, but I just passed it off, saying Roy and I had had words. We were pretty much ready to leave at that point, but it was late, so we went to bed, getting up early the next morning and ordering a taxi to take us and our stuff to Lucy's house to start, as I thought, our new lives together.

CHAPTER 9

I was now jobless. Even though Behrooz had told me he would keep me, it's not in my nature to be indolent out of work; I have always worked for my living. So, once our belongings were deposited at Lucy's, I started job hunting and accommodation hunting.

At that time, Kidderminster was still a big manufacturer of carpets, a town quite famous for carpets, Axminster, and all the well-known brands, but jobs were few and far between no matter what job role I tried. Due to the influx of students, most part-time jobs were taken by students, as employers could get away with paying students very little in the seventies. The same situation was true of accommodation; everywhere was full to overflowing. Good job Behrooz had known about Lucy.

After a conversation with Behrooz, I decided to go back to Coventry to look for work. It really did not sit well with me to be a kept woman. Behrooz would continue his studies at Kidderminster College; I would go back to Behrooz on weekends.

I found employment at the Chestford Grange, a big complex situated between Coventry and Leamington. It was a hotel with a nightclub, the 1812, where I frequented while seeing Robert. This hotel had just been bought by an Asian businessman called Chadbra; he also owned a hotel in Coventry. The Chestford Grange was a recent purchase; Chadbra was systematically revamping the whole complex. The architect who had the contract was actually living in at the Grange while the work was in progress.

My new role was as bars manageress over the seven bars situated in the hotel, nightclub, and function rooms.

There was a bar manager, Steve. He did not take kindly to gaining an assistant; his problem, not mine. Chadbra liked me, so Steve had to suck it up. I had explained to Chadbra that I was engaged, that my fiancé was at college in Kidderminster, and that on my days off I would go back to Kidderminster to visit him. On occasion, my fiancé would visit me in Coventry. Chadbra was quite happy for Behrooz to stay with me in staff accommodation, which was a little cottage situated just at the bottom of the lane the Grange stood on.

The cottage was a run-down dump with holes in the roof, but not in my room, which was on the ground floor. Chadbra was lashing money out on the hotel while the live-in staff, such as myself, lived in squalor. Every morning, I would walk up the lane to the hotel, where I would grab a bite to eat with the other staff before starting work. Meals and accommodation were part of our wages; I was entitled to three meals a day but rarely had more than one, not only because I did not eat much but because my stomach always seemed to be a bit upset lately. I had started to put weight on, which I really did not want to do as my wedding was not far away; no way was I going to pay to have my dress altered.

During the day, I would make sure all the bars were stocked with the items they needed for that day's work. Steve, the other bar manager, did the staff rotas. At that point, it worked well; going forward, it would be my place to start doing staff rotas as I was the newbie, being eased into the full manager role by Chadbra.

Chadbra was also aware of my forthcoming wedding to Behrooz, which was taking place in Kidderminster. My parents, by this point, had been introduced to Behrooz on one of my weekend trips home. To my surprise, my mother had not made any of her usual nasty comments about my current relationship, mainly, I think, because she had her hands full with my sister, who still lived at home with my niece, who was, at that time, five years old. My sister had been fifteen when she had gotten pregnant with my niece, going into premature labour at eight months after my younger sister, Rita, had caused a major incident by accusing her then-current boyfriend of raping her. Rita was, as I have said previously, a special needs child who ran away from home from an early age, causing all sorts of trouble whenever she could. Not only did her latest escapade cause such stress to Vicki that it brought on Sarah's early birth, but my dad had a serious heart condition, having suffered several heart attacks.

My sister Vicki, at this point, was just coming up to nineteen years old and was in a period of no longer wanting to be a mother to a nearly five-year-old child. She told my parents she was going to put Sarah up for adoption. My parents were furious; I can't say I blamed them for that, as both my parents had helped Vicki raise Sarah. My mother told my sister, "If anyone is going to adopt Sarah, it's me and your dad – that's our grandchild. It would have been different if you had said you wanted to have Sarah adopted at birth, but not after nearly five years of us loving our grandchild. And if you do try to get her adopted outside the family, you really don't think you're staying here, do you? To start gallivanting about all over the place before possibly ending up pregnant again?"

Sarah, my niece, was only four pounds when she was born, partly because of the premature birth and partly because her dad had had polio at a young age, which we now know contributed to Sarah's birth weight and to other defects, such as the fact that Sarah has only ever had one set of teeth in her life – no baby teeth being replaced by adult teeth as she grew. Sarah is now fifty-three years old, still with her only set of teeth, her baby teeth.

My parents and my sister were coming to Kidderminster for the wedding, which was taking place at the Kidderminster register office. My niece Sarah was going to be my bridesmaid.

So, as I knew all this stress at home and trying to plan a wedding while working a mile away from both the venue and my fiancé was taking its toll on me, I was always tired, not sleeping right, and even though I was limiting myself to one meal a day, my weight was fluctuating up and down like a yo-yo.

One night at work, just before I was due to go back to Kidderminster for the wedding, I was working the reception bar with another member of staff. It was massively busy with a big function taking place. As I served up a gin and tonic to a customer, I caught a whiff of the gin as I passed it to the customer, and my stomach churned. I put it down to my yo-yo diet and stress. I continued to work for a short while longer, serving drinks, until once again I served up another gin and tonic, with my stomach churning more violently this time.

I beckoned Steve over, telling him, "I don't feel well; take over while I pop to the loo." I rinsed my face with cold water, catching a breath of fresh air just outside the front door.

Once back at the bar, Steve told me that one of the other managers – a really nice chap I got along with – had had a difference of opinion with Chadbra that day and had been sacked. All the staff were going to the manager's room that night for a bit of a leaving party; did I want to come along? Saying yes, I thought, "Sure, what a shame it had come to this."

After the shift ended, we all made our way to the manager's room where quite a few staff were partying. There was not a lot of room for people to sit, so another couple of girls and I sat on the bed. I was reclining on the pillows along with another girl; I was dead tired and could feel myself starting to nod off, which I did. The next thing I knew, someone was shaking me awake. As I started up half asleep at the bottom of the bed, three of the male staff had dropped their trousers as a joke, waggling their bottoms at me. I was startled, struggling to get off the bed as the other girls were still sitting alongside me. In my disoriented, half-asleep state, with my history of being raped by Ken Greenwell, all I wanted was to get out of there as soon as possible.

The manager, who was leaving, caught hold of me, saying, "Chris, it's okay, come on, I will walk you home. You can't walk by yourself." I was very grateful for this, as I was still a bit shaken. Even though I was now fully awake and knew their prank was not meant seriously, they did not know my history. As we walked along the lane to my room, I started to calm down. The manager told me he was catching a taxi the next morning to Coventry train station to go back to his parents' home. As I was also catching the train that day to go back to Kidderminster, we agreed to share the taxi. The next morning, after about three hours of sleep, the taxi with the manager duly arrived, getting us to Coventry train station for the first train to Birmingham, where I changed trains for Kidderminster. The manager went for the London train taking him to his parents. We parted affably, promising to keep in touch.

Upon my arrival at Lucy's, Behrooz was surprised to see me so early in the morning. I explained the early train situation, not telling him anything about the prank, telling Behrooz to go to college while I sorted out the last few bits for the wedding.

The next morning, I had an appointment at the hairdressers; the wedding was booked for one in the afternoon. My parents, sister, and niece would arrive about noon, with Sarah already in her bridesmaid outfit, which I had bought her and which she was very excited about. We had invited Lucy and some of the lads who not only went to the same college as Behrooz but also had rooms at Lucy's to the wedding. One of them, Sandy, was a Scottish man doing a refresher course for his company. Sandy was a lovely man who had once called me stouter. I had asked, "What does that mean?" Sandy explained, "If you were an apple in a basket of apples, you would be the best beautiful apple among the baskets." What a lovely compliment from a lovely man. Also attending was my friend Heather, who had worked with me at the Wheel pub.

The wedding meal was booked for a local restaurant near the register office. On my arrival at the hairdressers, which I had never used before, the staff, although not busy, were very slow, not really paying attention to the customers. I had explained when I walked in that I was getting married in a couple of hours and how I wanted my hair to look. The stylist paid no attention to my requests at all; in fact, she kept wandering off on various excuses, almost as if she were purposely determined to make me late. And no, I was not being a bridezilla.

In the end, I got really stroppy, telling the stylist to hurry up. She finished my hair, asking me if my hair was okay. At that point, I had not seen my style, not being positioned in front of a mirror. I was appalled at the style she had given me; it was nothing anywhere near what I had asked for. By now, the wedding was imminent. I raced from the hairdressers to the taxi rank around the corner, only to be confronted by a line of people waiting for cabs. I never gave it a thought, standing in front of the line and saying, "I'm going to be really cheeky; I'm due to get married in twenty minutes. I've been held up at the hairdressers and the dry cleaners. Please can I jump the queue? Will anyone mind?" Do you know whether it was my distressed state or the fact that by now I was nearly in tears, but not one person had a problem with me getting the next cab that came in. With hindsight, maybe this was the universe's way of telling me, "Don't be a fool; out of the frying pan, into the fire," who knows.

The taxi deposited me back at Lucy's, where everyone was waiting, panicking, and wondering where I had gotten to. Within fifteen minutes, I was dressed, the appalling hairstyle ripped out and brushed into the style I had wanted all along, and off to the registry office.

I now know I really should have listened to all the omens the universe was throwing at me, but as the ceremony went ahead, I thought I had found my happily ever after. Boy, was I wrong.

After the wedding and subsequent meal, my parents, sister, and niece left to go back home, while my new husband and I, along with the lads who rented from Lucy, made our way back to Lucy's guesthouse.

The next morning, Behrooz and I walked into Kidderminster to do a bit of shopping. Later that night, we went to the local pub. I still had another day of leave before going back to work at the Grange. Behrooz was on college break for another week, so he decided to come back to the Grange with me for a couple of days. Chadbra had previously met Behrooz, so upon arrival at the Grange, Chadbra asked Behrooz if he wanted to do a couple of jobs around the Grange to help out, which Behrooz agreed to.

A couple of days later, Behrooz had to go back to college. We had arranged to go to the college's Christmas do when I got back to Kidderminster, along with Maggie and Amhad. I was quite excited about it, never having been to anything like it before, but had heard these Christmas events were amazing.

On the night of the event, Behrooz and I taxied to the college, meeting Maggie and Amhad there. The men went up to the bar to get drinks, leaving us girls chatting away.

All of a sudden, a couple of male students armed with mistletoe grabbed Maggie and me, asking for kisses. I said no, my husband would not like that. Maggie, however, gave her student a smacker, turning to me and saying it's all a bit of fun. So, when the men came back from the bar, Maggie told Amhad what had happened. Behrooz grabbed me, saying, "Where is he? You're hiding him." I was shocked, and to be honest, so was Maggie. She told Behrooz not to be so silly, again repeating it's just a bit of Christmas high spirits.

That seemed to calm Behrooz down. A short while later, once again, the men went to buy drinks. Within a few seconds, the same student who had asked me for a kiss suddenly reappeared, grabbing me and asking for a kiss. All of a sudden, he was knocked on his backside as Behrooz appeared from nowhere, shouting, "That's my wife!" I don't know who was more stunned: me, the student, or Maggie and Amhad, who stepped between Behrooz and the student, arms out, telling Behrooz to calm down. All this happened within seconds. In fact, I did not realise until Amhad stepped between the two men that I was actually holding my breath with shock and embarrassment.

Behrooz turned on me, grabbed me by the arm, and dragged me out to a taxi, all the while yelling and shouting, telling me I was a whore and using other choice words. The tirade continued on the short ride back to Lucy's. Once inside, I just started to throw my belongings into my suitcase, telling Behrooz I had done nothing wrong. "The way you have just treated me was disgusting. If you think I'm staying here, you're wrong."

That gave Behrooz pause; he instantly became contrite, begging and wheedling, telling me he was so in love with me he just flipped. My reply was, "That's no excuse. Amhad did not have that reaction to Maggie giving her student a kiss, while I did not even kiss the one asking me. It's all Christmas high jinks."

At that point, Behrooz grabbed me, kissed me, and cried, telling me he couldn't live without me – a maelstrom of emotions. He persuaded me he was contrite and that it would not happen again. So, I stayed. To be honest, as it was late at night and Christmas in a one-horse town, I had nowhere to go anyway; there was no way I could get back to Coventry. Even if I had, my mother sure as hell would not be happy to let me stay with them. The next day, Behrooz was still contrite, going out of his way to prove his words.

The following days were all calm; my holiday was coming to an end, and my return to the Grange was imminent. Behrooz had broken up from college for the Christmas break; the college Christmas party had marked the end of term. We were going to my parents' house for Christmas Day after my last shift at the Grange on Christmas Eve; my dad was picking us up from the Grange. At that point, my health was not great; I had been very tired and off my food. I put it down to overwork, late hours, and early mornings – all associated with working in the hotel and pub trade.

We stayed at my parents' house after Christmas dinner for a couple of days, with my first shift back at the Grange not being until the following week. My mother suggested that while I was off and not feeling great, I should visit the doctor for a check-up, which I did. My doctor had known me since I was a child. During the check-up, he commented on my wedding ring, saying it was nice to see I was remarried and reminding me not to forget to give reception my new details. He was looking at me in quite a funny way. In my previous marriage, I had undergone all sorts of tests to find out why I could not conceive a child; the results had shown that I would never be able to have children. Dr Bowman then said I was looking quite "blousy", and while I was there, maybe we should do an internal exam just to make sure everything was well.

This did shock me in a way, but back in the day, you did not question your doctor; they were like gods – see all, hear all.

The exam took only seconds. Dr Bowman helped me down from the table, saying, "Congratulations, you're pregnant."

"What!

"Hang on a second, Dr Bowman, you know very well that's not possible".

Dr Bowman smiled, saying, "Christine, in my many years of practice, I have seen many wonders. You are about eight weeks along, but we will do a water test to confirm."

He sent me home, saying I would get appointments through the post for ante-natal and other pregnancy-related bits.

I left his office thinking to myself, he's gone barmy in his old age; I can't be pregnant – it's just not possible, and the water test will prove I am not pregnant.

Upon my arrival home, my mother asked me how my appointment had gone. I filled her in, telling both her and Behrooz it's just not possible. I had told Behrooz about my previous marriage and the fact I could not have children; he had assured me it did not matter to him as he loved me.

Plus, apart from feeling tired and not having much of an appetite, there were no other signs of pregnancy, such as morning sickness or tender breasts, etc.

The next day, Behrooz went back to college. I was due to go back to the Grange that weekend. Unusually, my mother was being nice to me for a change, so staying at my parents' house was not too much of a chore. Due to my recent marriage, there was quite a bit of paperwork that needed to be done – name changes at various official departments within the city. In those days, there were no emails; it was all by footfall. So, for the next couple of days, that's what I did – walking miles.

Meeting up with some friends and reminiscing while in Coventry, on my return to my mother's on the second day after Behrooz went back to college, Dr Bowman rang me, saying, "Your test results are back;

you're confirmed as about eight weeks pregnant." Denial is a great thing. My mother was telling me to rest; my reply was, "Dr Bowman is wrong; so is the test." Leaving the conversation at that point, I went to the loo, where I found my underwear covered in blood. I shouted down to my sister, asking her to bring me a sanitary pad, saying I knew Dr Bowman was wrong. The next thing I knew, my mother flew into the bathroom, saying, "For God's sake, you idiot, you're having a miscarriage; get into bed. I'm ringing for Dr Bowman to come out."

That shocked me and stunned me. My nan, who was now living with my mother, came to me, saying, "Come on, love, do as you're told; get into bed." Once my nan said that, awareness finally landed. Dr Bowman duly arrived, examining me, and telling both my mother and Nan, "The cervix is wide open; the foetus can come away any time."

That was the point when realisation finally penetrated my brain: I'm pregnant!

Along with realisation came determination and stubbornness. This baby is going nowhere for another seven months. Dr Bowman prescribed bed rest, giving me something to aid my rest. Saying, "Stay in bed; I'm at a medical conference over the weekend. I will check back with you after that. If anything happens, call an ambulance."

My mother phoned the Grange, telling them what was going on, saying, "As soon as we know what's happening, we will inform you of a return-to-work date."

On Monday morning, my situation was the same – in bed but with no more bleeding, which was a good sign. Dr Bowman arrived that afternoon, telling me about this new drug given to women in Germany in my situation. It was still experimental but had produced good results in German women, saving many pregnancies. Would I consider trying it?

No Brainer!

Of course, I would if it saved my baby. Dr Bowman went on to say the district nurse would have to come in every week to give me this drug by injection in the buttocks, and I would still have to have total bed rest.

The next day, a district nurse duly turned up with the drug in a glass phial. It took forever to draw up into the syringe as it was a really thick substance. The nurse said she had never administered this drug before, and as she tried to administer it, the thickness made it take forever to inject and was really painful, leaving a massive bruise.

The following week, when the nurse arrived, she said she had been asking for advice around administration. The consensus was to heat the drug up to thin the substance, which made it easier to draw up into the syringe and subsequently into my buttocks. Thank god it was not so painful that time, and there was no detriment to the drug's physiology.

No more massive bruises: this went on for another five months. My backside was like a used dartboard at the end of treatment, but it saved my baby.

Years later, this treatment was discontinued as it was found to make the children born after the use of this drug aggressive, and the mothers subsequently had sciatic nerve issues.

I often wonder now if maybe this treatment caused, in some way, my daughter's rapid cycling bipolar.

We will never know for sure.

Another side effect of this regime of drugs and bed rest was weight gain, as I had gone from being extremely active to a full stop. It took me about a year after the birth of my daughter to lose the weight, but I was never back to my pre-pregnancy weight – another side effect of the drug.

During my pregnancy, Behrooz finished college, giving notice to Lucy, and moving into my mother's house to look after me. Obviously, my Grange job had also ended. My dad went with Behrooz to pick up all my belongings from the hotel. Behrooz, at that point, was still getting money from his parents obstensibly for his college fees but was now using it to cover our stay, room, and board at my mother's while he looked for work. Behrooz still had not told his parents he had married, which was causing me emotional distress, as I wondered why he did not want to tell them about the woman he said he loved and the child they were expecting. Behrooz's dad was a high-ranking colonel in the Shah's army, and his brother was chief of police in Tehran. Behrooz had done his national service prior to attending college and had stated right from our first meeting that there was no way he was going back to Iran.

Another thing that was upsetting me was that there was no physical contact from Behrooz at all during my pregnancy; his excuse was that, because of the delicacy of my pregnancy, he was scared to be intimate. At that time, I believed him.

As my pregnancy progressed, due to being on constant bed rest, I missed out on all antenatal appointments and birth classes, having to rely on my mother and my sister to fill me in on what to expect.

Behrooz was really trying hard to find work without much luck.

One day it was just Behrooz and me in the house, the rest of the family having gone out, when the front doorbell rang. I was in bed upstairs, and Behrooz answered the door to find one of his fellow students on the doorstep along with his dad, who was visiting from Iran.

Behrooz came upstairs, telling me he was going to pop out with them and that he would be back shortly. I was a bit startled, expecting Behrooz to at least tell them something to the effect of having to see to his wife before going out, but it was so fast I never got the chance. To be fair, he was not gone for long. When he came back, I asked him why he had not told them about me or mentioned his wife upstairs. His explanation was that the student and his dad, who had turned up at our house, were best friends with his dad back in Iran. Behrooz did not want anyone to tell his dad about his wife before he got the chance to tell his dad himself, which at the time seemed a plausible explanation.

As I have stated several times, at that time, I was really naive and in love.

From what I had learned up to this point about Muslim men in general, they were the power in any family, with women taking second place. In fact, one Muslim man had told me while still at the Park Attwood that women and dogs have no souls, and women must follow ten steps behind any man.

This had shocked me to the core, but Behrooz, up until now, had not seemed to follow that doctrine, seeming very westernised.

This situation with the student who had arrived at my mum's house, whose name was Mo, gave me doubt, especially as being bed-bound, I was feeling very vulnerable anyway.

Behrooz assured me that Mo's dad was going back to Iran in a couple of days. Once his dad was gone, Mo would visit Behrooz and would be told about me, which did happen.

My pregnancy was by now nearing the end, so I was allowed out of bed for a good few hours a day. I will never forget the first time I felt my baby move. I was sitting in the lounge during one of my allowed out-of-bed slots when all of a sudden, from my navel up towards my breasts, there was a feeling of someone trailing a feather inside my body, startling me, and making me let out a little squeal of surprise. My mother rushed over, thinking I was in trouble. I said no, telling her what I had just felt. Mum said, "That's your baby's first movement."

Mo had continued to visit Behrooz, during which time it became more and more clear that Behrooz was very reticent to tell Mo I was, in fact, his wife. Until the day my sister, seeing how upset the situation was making me, gave Behrooz a good broadside, telling him either he puts Mo in the picture, or she will the next time he visits. Behrooz had confessed to me that Mo thought Behrooz was renting a room from my family, which appalled me. In my vulnerable state, did this mean Behrooz was ashamed of me? Was he using me to gain British citizenship? All kinds of thoughts were going through my head.

As I knew from the Park Attwood days, some of the Iranian students there had done just that with girls they were seeing.

Behrooz assured me and my family that the next time Mo visited, he would divulge everything to him.

As it happened, the next time Mo visited, our baby – a daughter – had been born after a very complicated birth where I had been knocked out of labour by a nurse administering painkillers before asking me if I had any pain, then having to restart my labour again by making me drink jug after jug of glucose, which has the effect on the uterus of continuing labour.

At the end of that labour, the midwife offered me a cup of tea, which I gratefully accepted. As glucose is sickly sweet, I needed something to take away the taste. Unfortunately, the tea on top of all that glucose had the effect of something akin to a good Saturday night out on the booze. I threw up for England all over the place, as the midwife had left the sick bowl on the other bed in my room, and I could not reach it. By the time she came back into my room, not only was I covered, but the bed and floor were covered in a thick, viscous liquid of tea and glucose. The midwife said, "Oh my God, you look like you have had a good night out on the town." My reply: "I wish I had; it would have been a lot easier."

In those days after a birth, women stayed in the hospital for five days, unlike today, where hospitals throw you out after a few hours due to not only being underfunded but also the increase in birth rate, making it more of a production line.

On my release from the hospital, we returned to my mother's house. I am eternally grateful for the help I had there from my sister, but now, after my daughter's birth, my mother was reverting to her old ways, making my life a misery.

Behrooz had finally gotten a job working as a porter at Walsgrave Hospital, and we were desperately house hunting. In those days, the late seventies, you did not need a deposit for a house, getting what was termed a hundred percent mortgage.

This was when Mo visited. My sister let him in as I was in the middle of changing my daughter, having just fed her. Behrooz was sitting on the sofa, watching me tend to our daughter.

They started chatting away in Farsi. My sister came into the lounge, asking Mo if he would like a cup of tea while giving Behrooz a glare, as up to that point, both men had totally ignored me and the baby. Mo said he would love a cup of tea; my sister duly served Mo his tea but stood in the doorway of the lounge, pointedly glaring at Behrooz. Behrooz switched to English, saying to Mo, "You see that there," pointing at me, "that's mine". Not 'that's my wife,' just 'that's mine,' "and you see that there," pointing at our daughter, "that's mine as well."

Devastated at the way Behrooz had introduced me to Mo and devastated at the way Behrooz had told Mo about our baby, but relieved he had told Mo, the situation was saved by Mo's surprise; you could see his delight at the fact that Behrooz had a daughter. Seconds after his shock subsided, he clasped my hands, saying how pleased he was to meet me and what a beautiful child we had. But it left a really nasty taste in my mouth, as it was blatantly obvious that if not for my sister, Behrooz would not have told Mo.

After Mo left, my sister confronted Behrooz, telling him exactly what she thought of him, which mirrored my thoughts and feelings exactly. How could he be so nasty? Was I right in thinking I was being used as a foothold to his citizenship? However, later that night, Behrooz actually sat down and wrote to his parents, enclosing photos of our baby, telling them he was married and would not be returning to Iran. I was delighted.

But, sad to say, this was all part of the manipulation I was to experience in the rest of my marriage; this man was a consummate manipulator and narcissist.

Bear in mind at this point, I had a new baby, my husband was working, and we were house hunting. So yet again, his handling of telling family and friends about his new family was put down to his culture and the way Muslim men handled situations and my naivety.

CHAPTER 10

Some six months later, we had bought our first house in Dame Agnes Grove, Bell Green, for six thousand pounds. I was ecstatic. I persuaded my mother to babysit while I went and cleaned and decorated the house to a reasonable standard to allow us to move in. A nurse at the hospital where Behrooz now worked gave Behrooz her second-hand cooker, which my dad screwed to the kitchen wall as the top was broken, but it worked. My nan gave us two old chairs to sit on and loaned me the money to buy a carpet for the lounge. Luckily, the previous owner of the house had left curtains and floor covering in the bedrooms. We took out a Mutual loan to buy a bed, the only new bit of furniture we owned. I had a few old crocks from my nan and a couple of old battered pans again from my nan, no television, or any form of entertainment apart from a few books saved from my childhood. But as Behrooz seemed happy and content working and doing overtime as often as he could, I actually thought all my dreams of a man who loved me, and a rosy future had finally come true.

As the days wore on, Behrooz's wage, which was paltry as a porter and only just covered the monthly mortgage without overtime, started giving cause for concern, little things at first.

Such as I only had a pound a week to buy fruit and vegetables to make meals; luckily there was a veg shop in Bell Green Centre where you could go along late in the day to pick up battered stuff that most people wouldn't buy. But harkening back to my childhood in Hillfields, when Dad had lost his job and money was scarce, stood me in good stead for making meals out of nothing. There was a Sainsbury's in the shopping centre, but no way could I afford their prices. We did not eat meat – it was too expensive – so our dinners consisted of veg, pasta, and potatoes with dumplings of various sorts to fill us up. Nearly back to good old giblet stew, but not quite.

I prided myself on being a really good cook; what we ate was tasty with the use of herbs and spices, all gleaned from my Polish background.

Behrooz was starting to be really snappy at home, just little things which I put down to tiredness after a long day at work. I was still in the era when men went to work and women cared for their man when he got home, although I was bone-tired myself from caring for our daughter. Aslin was a fretful baby, as I now know due to the treatment we had received during my pregnancy. On top of doing all the housework, I walked into town and back to pay bills – no online methods in those days – and we could not afford bus fares. While in town visiting the market, there were times when, if you haggled and were wise, you could buy three times as much for my weekly pound as I could get in the veg shop near me. Still, in the seventies, few little shops had refrigeration, so they would sell off any items that were delicate as the last thing before closing cheaply. There were times at the market I had managed to get some really cheap meat – nothing most people would eat, offal and the like or dodgy sausages – okay if used that night and a rare treat.

We were so hard up that I was wearing Behrooz's old underpants as my pants were all worn out and now used as rags. The clothes that I managed to buy were all from jumble sales. Gone were the days when I could afford to shop in the town dress shops, thinking nothing of how much a nice dress cost. These days, my daughter came first. I was lucky my sister's child was five years older than Aslin, so I inherited everything Sarah outgrew.

Although it was a struggle, I managed all the house finances, never getting into debt – a real "Rob Peter to pay Paul" time. Behrooz would have nothing to do with the finances; he told me I was the woman of the house, and it was my duty to sort out everything to do with the home. In a way, I accepted that as my mother had also been in charge of everything to do with the home.

Now, years later, I realise my mother wore the trousers in our family and had my dad under her thumb, while Behrooz, coming from his culture where men ruled the women, expected to be treated like a god with no expectations of ever having to do anything in the home except eat, sleep, and have sex on demand. In other words, I was his slave. So, I had traded my childhood as a slave to my mother for an adult life as my husband's slave. When you are in a relationship, you just don't realise what exactly is good and bad about it; you just carry on thinking you can work out all the problems and issues, that things will get better. You carry on and on, and before you know it, you are conditioned to things being the way they are.

Behrooz by now would come home from work, expect his dinner to be on the table ready when he walked in the door, totally ignore his child, and fall asleep on the floor in front of the fire.

Aslin, by this point, was about a year old. I decided enough was enough, telling Behrooz I would be looking for a part-time job. He really did not like that, telling me he was the breadwinner. My reply: your wages are a pittance even when you can get overtime. It won't hurt me to do a couple of nights a week for a few hours somewhere. As it happened, the petrol station just up the road was advertising for a part-time cashier for a couple of hours two nights a week. I applied and got the job.

I now realise Behrooz did not want to have to take care of his daughter while I was out at work. I would put Aslin to bed before I went out at six o'clock; within minutes, she would be asleep, and when I got back at ten o'clock, she would still be asleep, so it's not as if Behrooz was having anything to do for his daughter.

The little bit of money I brought home made my life a lot easier, enabling me to stop trawling around shops for dodgy veg and, once a week, buying a bit of meat.

Behrooz sulked for about two weeks, but then he seemed to accept his dogmatic ways were not going to change anything for him, as I was now determined to stop being a doormat and make things easier for myself and my child.

I worked at that petrol station for around six months before leaving to return to pub work, getting a job two nights a week waitressing, at which I was damn good. I could make fifteen pounds a night in tips – more than my wages for two nights – and a hell of a lot of money in the seventies.

One night, the manageress asked me if the following week I could do some day shifts as well as my regular nights since the Royal Show was on, which would bring in quite a bit of trade. I told her yes but never said a word to Behrooz about the extra shifts, as I knew he wouldn't like me doing them. Even then, I never realised it was all about control. So, I asked my sister if she would watch Aslin; she said of course, no problem.

I duly worked the extra shifts I had been asked to do, which reaped me quite a lot of extra tips, getting the Pub Manageress to put the extra shifts through over a couple of weeks' pay slips. One, so Behrooz would not know I had done them, and two, stopping the taxman from taking away all my extra money earned in income tax, the bastards. The extra money I had earned enabled me to buy for our dinner that weekend and, on the Saturday night, two steaks, which I did with chips, mushrooms, and salad – something we had not had in nearly two years – and a nice bit of beef for Sunday dinner, something we had never had. Behrooz thought he was so clever, but never questioned how we had come to be able to afford meat and beef that we had two days on the trot. I was so excited to be able to serve my family a decent dinner from my earnings.

Behrooz worked a half-day every Saturday. That night, as I prepared our meal, Behrooz was in the garden pottering about. He had been really quiet since arriving home from work around one o'clock that day; as usual, I put it down to tiredness. I took extra care to present our meal on the plate, so it was appealing to the eye as well as the stomach, calling Behrooz in from the garden, telling him dinner was ready. Aslin had been quite fretful that day, suffering from a summer cold. As Behrooz came in, he snapped at me, saying, "Has she had her dinner?" I said, "No, she's a bit off today with this cold." He snapped again, saying, "Well, you better sort her out as I want to enjoy my dinner without a brat screaming down my ear while I'm trying to eat."

Shocked, I looked at him, saying, "One, she's not a brat; she's your child. Two, I don't know what's upset you today, but don't take it out on us. Aslin will sit at the table with us; we are a family, and we will eat together. I'm sure she will settle once we sit down." At that point, Aslin used to sit by me in her highchair for meals; I would help her to eat certain foods while I ate my own meals.

Behrooz slammed his cup down on the counter he had been holding, saying, "If you're putting that brat before me, you can shove your dinner."

Shock upon shock.

Absolutely no reason for the tirade I was now experiencing. I said to Behrooz, "Please calm down; I have made this dinner special as I got a bit extra in tips this week," still not divulging my extra shifts. "I've bought some rump steak, look."

The next thing I knew, Behrooz stormed off up to the top of the garden, standing with his arms folded and a face like thunder. Aslin, by now, was screaming due to Behrooz's ranting and raving, upsetting an already fretful child.

I put Aslin in her highchair, giving her some dinner to start eating. I then went up the garden to Behrooz, at this point still unaware just how mad he was and not knowing why. As I approached, I said, "Behrooz, I have no idea what's gone on with you today, but you are being ridiculous." He looked at me with pure, unadulterated hate, turning his back on me and staying silent with his arms folded.

Stupefied, I looked at his rigid back and face full of hate, then turned and left him to it, thinking, for fuck's sake, just get on with it, whatever it is.

I returned to my child, who by now was calm and spooning her dinner into her mouth. I put a lid over Behrooz's dinner, thinking once the idiot man calmed down, it would be there ready for him to eat. I ate my dinner, which really tasted like ash in my mouth after Behrooz's tantrum, but I was determined not to waste a meal we rarely got.

After dinner, I put Aslin to bed. Behrooz was still in his rigid position in the garden. Late that night, I went to bed; yes, Behrooz was still standing like a glowering sentinel in the garden.

The next morning, being Sunday, when I woke, you're not going to believe this, Behrooz was still in the same spot in the garden, covered in dew and cobwebs. What an absolute raving asshole.

Now, I was as mad as hell. What an absolute knob. Now, with hindsight, which is a marvellous thing, that should have been my wake-up call, what with his snappy attitude over the past few months and then this tirade.

But as everyone knows, love is blind. When you're in a relationship, you always think things will work out.

A short while after getting up and seeing to Aslin, I made a cup of tea. As I did, Behrooz walked in the back door, saying, "Have you made me a cup?"

as if nothing had happened and he had not been standing in the garden all night like a stupid scarecrow – only scarier.

Trying to keep things light, I said no, but as I was making tea, I made him a cup, which he took, chatting away to his daughter as if nothing had happened.

Bemused? Much! Hell yes, but not wanting a repeat, I left it alone.

Later that day, Aslin was down for a nap. I tackled Behrooz, saying, "What the hell was that all about yesterday? If you want your dinner, it's under a plate; I kept it for you. When we were children, if we refused our meals, Mum would serve it up until we ate it, as we were being naughty children, and food is not cheap."

Behrooz did no more than pick up the plate with his dinner on it and threw it across the room at me, saying, "Carry on if you dare." I was shaken to the core. Where was the man I had married, who seemed loving and caring? This man standing before me now was the Kidderminster incident man who had gone berserk with that student.

Growing up in the fifties, children watched and heard many a row like this between married couples, often seeing wives walking around with black eyes from their men. Now, in the seventies, was I to become such a wife? Although I did not know it at that point, yes, I was.

By now, I was trembling, shaken but not wanting our daughter to see or hear anything going on. I kept my mouth shut and stayed away from Behrooz.

Aslin woke from her nap, and I tended to her while Behrooz carried on as if nothing had happened. I made dinner, which he ate without mentioning the fact that we were eating beef. How had I afforded it? Nothing.

For the next few weeks, I was on tenterhooks, constantly, in case of another rampage, but it all remained quiet on the western front!

This is how narcissists work: control freaks. They watch like silent killers – and sadly a lot actually do murder their partners. They bide their time, waiting for you to settle after an incident; it's like a cobra waiting to strike. Just when you think everything is going to be all right is when they strike.

Our life continued without incident for some time, but Behrooz was becoming more dominant, done in such a way you don't realise at the time, little things like stopping you from going across the road to chat with your neighbour with a plausible excuse as to why they need you at home at that moment.

Asking you what you have been doing all day, then dropping in, "Well, if that's all you have done today, why hasn't this been done?"

Our first wedding anniversary had been such an example. My parents had said they would babysit if we wanted to go out for a meal. I arranged to go to the Royal Court, very deluxe. Behrooz said no, we will go out when Aslin has grown up. I thought he was joking; so, did my parents. They encouraged me to book the meal out. On the day, Behrooz went begrudgingly but couldn't make a scene in front of my parents. When we got to the Royal Court, the barmaid asked Behrooz to wear a tie. I had no idea there was a dress code. He went mad, saying, "Right, we are going home." After the Kidderminster incident, I just went, arriving back home an hour after leaving, starving hungry, to bemused babysitting parents. Needless to say, Behrooz stormed off to bed, leaving me to say goodnight to my parents and then making myself some toast before going to bed, where Behrooz was snoring away.

Then there were the numerous occasions where friends and neighbours would invite us out for drinks or meals. I would ask Behrooz; he would say yes, then at the last-minute take overtime, meaning he couldn't go, or say he was too tired, didn't feel well, and the excuses carried on. To the stage that one of my friends told me, "We won't ask you out anymore. We make plans; you always cancel at the last minute," so effectively Behrooz killed any chance of a social life at all.

Then the second wedding anniversary, my dad took Behrooz aside, telling him in no uncertain terms he would take me out for a meal and that my parents, once again, would babysit, which I did not know anything about until after the event. Behrooz told me we were going out for our anniversary. I was more than surprised and pleased, but also wary after the first anniversary debacle.

So, I told Behrooz I really hope this is for real, you're not winding me up. He assured me no, I mean it, not divulging my dad's part in the setting up of this outing.

We went to the Sunflower House, a Chinese restaurant by the Coventry train station, after a couple of drinks in a local pub, which again surprised me as Behrooz was not one for taking me out for a drink. As we walked into the restaurant, I was wearing a black suit held over from my pre-married days, which I looked really nice in. There was a table of chaps to my right-hand side that we had to pass by to get to our table. One of the chaps wolf-whistled at me as I passed by; I had not even made eye contact with any of them as I had my arm linked in Behrooz's. In an instant, Behrooz flew at this chap. I still had my arm linked in Behrooz's, so I managed to tug him back, saying, "What the hell?" He was ranting, saying, "That cunt just whistled at you." My reply was, "So what? I did nothing to warrant that, so calm the hell down; you're being an idiot, everybody is looking at you." That gave Behrooz pause. He stopped, turning away from the table of lads, and carrying on to the table we were being shown to. To be honest, that surprised me, as I expected an onslaught of anger to be directed at me, innocent though I was. We had a nice meal, even though I was on high alert. We went home, and nothing more was said. Again, I was thinking, "Wow! This is a turnaround; finally, Behrooz is returning to the man I married." I don't know if Behrooz thought that upon arriving back home I would tell my dad about his flare-up in the restaurant, but I enjoyed a period of calm after that anniversary.

Then, the day I cashed in an insurance policy I had been saving since age sixteen, I was thrilled to have a bit of extra cash. I knew exactly what I was going to do with that cash: buy Aslin some new clothes instead of hand-me-downs from my sister.

Behrooz and I went into town, where I proceeded to buy Aslin the things I could never buy her before.

In one shop, I was so happy and excited to be buying my daughter a few new little dresses, asking Behrooz, "Which do you like best, these two, or shall I get both?" He turned on me in front of the lady serving me, saying, "I really don't give a fuck, just hurry the fuck up. I'm fed up now and want to go home." I could feel myself shrivel up with embarrassment and humiliation, turning red-faced to the cashier and saying, "Thank you, I will just take this one, please." In one second, Behrooz had ruined all my enjoyment and humiliated me on top of that. As we left the shop, he then compounded that embarrassment and humiliation by saying, "Now I want to go look around Owen and Owen." My reply was, "Okay, you go," considering what you just did to me in that shop, saying you were tired and fed up and wanting to go home. "Go on your own; I'm getting a taxi and going home." He was stunned, but my back was up. I crossed the road to the taxi rank. The next thing I knew, he was getting into the taxi with me, silent all the way home, giving me what I would come to know as the death stare. Surprisingly, once home, he seemed calm and sane.

But it was, I now realise, looking back over the years, a pattern of calm for a couple of weeks, then a flare-up over the most trivial of things, such as not putting a spoon back in the exact same place it had been before.

I do not know if any of you readers have ever watched the film with Julia Roberts, Sleeping with the Enemy, but her husband in that film, played by Patrick Bergin, could have been the exact character role my husband was taken from in real life.

By now, Aslin was two years old, and I was pregnant with our second child, once again facing a bad pregnancy requiring bed rest. It was difficult with a toddler running about the place, but I managed.

Behrooz once again refused to be intimate during the pregnancy but did man up and help out at home with cooking and other chores, my mother and sister also helping out.

When I went into labour, my mother took us to the hospital while Dad watched Aslin. My labour was prolonged and hard, lasting nearly three days until the hospital realised there was a problem, resulting in me having to have a ventouse extraction. Basically, they sucked the baby out, leaving a triangle-shaped lump on John's head (chignon), meaning I could not wash his hair for three months. This form of delivery is still used nowadays; back then, it was new, meaning before I knew it, my room was full of observers. But at that point, all I cared about was my baby's safety, not my dignity. It turned out my son had been lying the wrong way around, so I would never have been able to deliver him naturally.

Behrooz was thrilled to have a son. I knew Muslim men thought boys were the be-all and end-all in their world, but until you see them with a boy child, you just can't imagine the reality.

Once back home with our new baby, Behrooz could not do enough for us. Once again, all my hopes and aspirations seemed within reach.

Aslin had her own room in the house; there was a spare bedroom, then our shared bedroom. For the first few weeks, John was in a cot in our room for night feeds, etc. He was a really good baby, like chalk and cheese from Aslin, who had been a real fractious child. You could set the clock by John waking for feeds and nappy changes. Behrooz had taken two weeks' paternity leave from the hospital to help me; however, within a couple of days, Behrooz was back to his old habit of sleeping on the floor in front of the fire while I did everything. I remember one day standing, washing with my Servis twin tub in the kitchen while cooking dinner and rocking John in his pram with one foot while trying to entertain Aslin in her baby bouncer, all at the same time as Behrooz totally ignored his entire family, flat out on the lounge floor, snoring.

May as well have been on my own; basically, I really was. And now, again looking back, I really would have made a better job of raising a family on my own without Behrooz's interfering emotional and physical abuse.

Just before Behrooz was due back to work from his paternity leave during the night, John had woken for his feed. I don't know what time it must have been as there was no clock in our bedroom. I had fed him, changed him, and unusually he was a bit fretful afterwards, so I put him in the bed with me to soothe him. As I did, Behrooz came into the room. Looking at his wife and child in our bed – John had put his little hand out as he drifted off, resting it on my face. I did not disturb him, waiting for him to gain a deep sleep before moving him back to his cot – Behrooz stood at the foot of the bed, staring at us, saying, "So it seems you really love this child then." I looked at him, replying, "I love both of my children."

That was the moment all our lives changed for the worst, which was the pivotal point. Behrooz's intense jealousy of his own children, for lack of a better understanding of his mental state, drove him insane with jealousy. It's the only way I can describe the change in him from that day on. Yes, there had been flare-ups such as the Kidderminster student and the anniversary meal, but nothing could prepare me for the intense leap in control, emotional abuse, and physical abuse I would suffer from that day on.

The next morning, after his remark about loving this child more than my other child, we rose early. Behrooz was due back to work that day. I was in the loo with the baby in my arms. Behrooz came into the bathroom and started to kiss me. I thought it was because he was going out to work shortly and would be missing his family, until he began getting amorous. Bearing in mind it was only two weeks since I had given birth and I was still bleeding while holding a newborn in my arms with very little way of defending myself, I managed to wriggle away for an instant, saying, "What the hell are you doing? I have our child in my arms." His facial expression was blank, his eyes like black stones – flat, no emotion, stone cold. He put his hands around my neck, squeezing hard. I couldn't breathe as I clawed at his hand with one of my hands while trying to protect John held in my other arm. I managed to cry out as Behrooz said in a cold, hard, flat voice, "There's no love left for me, is there, Chris?"

Aslin came to the bottom of the stairs, shouting up to us, aged nearly three years old, "Dad, what are you doing to Mummy?" Startled, he released his grip. I threw myself down the stairs, child in arms, gathering her up into the lounge, then the kitchen, locking the kitchen door behind us all.

I heard the front door slam as Behrooz left the house. It was only at that point I realised I was still holding my breath.

I honestly cannot describe the overwhelming cascade of emotion that hit me at that point. My first care was for the children as I flew to the front door, locking the door behind Behrooz, then tending to my children. Shaken, terrified, and helpless, I had nowhere to turn and no one to help me. I was trying to think about what was best to do. I knew my mother would not help; she had always made that crystal clear. My dad would have taken Behrooz on, but his health was very fragile, having suffered three heart attacks, so he was in no fit state to help.

As the day wore on, I watched the clock, waiting for Behrooz to return home, fearful of what would happen next.

Behrooz walked through the door as if nothing had happened, going straight to his son's crib, taking him out and cuddling him. Not a word of apology – nothing. He came over to me, putting his arms around me. I stood rigid with a meat hammer in my hand, used to tenderise steak. What use it would have been, I don't know, but in the moment,

I thought it would be some sort of deterrent to a homicidal maniac – it would not have been!

He kissed me on the cheek, asking what's for dinner. No apology, nothing – a totally different person.

I did not know what to do; being wary was an understatement. I spent the whole of that night like a cat on a hot tin roof, waiting for the cobra to strike again, not trusting Behrooz one inch. Every movement he made could have been a precursor to another attack. But no, things were very calm. From that moment, I was always on high alert, which, when you're in that situation, you really do not realise – you are on constant alert. It's absolutely draining, wearing away at your cognitive thinking, which, again, you don't realise.

A few days after the attack, I tried to tell Behrooz how he had terrified his family and that if it happened again, we would be gone. He told me he had no idea what I was going on about, that I had had a nightmare or a bad dream. Again, women in abusive relationships are made to believe by their abuser that any given situation that arises is all their own doing, their fault – typical Dr Jekyll and Mr Hyde.

CHAPTER 11

For a good time after that, things went along really well.

Behrooz, at that point, did not drive. Across the road from us lived a chap who ran a driving school. I paid for Behrooz to take driving lessons, but, as with any other social event, Behrooz would come up with excuses to avoid taking these lessons. So, I thought, "Bugger this," and I took them instead, passing my test on the first try. Over the years, I had saved a pound a week in a child's bank account for the two children. Once I passed my test, I used the couple of hundred quid in that account to buy a second-hand Mini, so it benefited me, the children, and Behrooz, as now the children and I could go on picnics, swimming, etc., while Behrooz was at work. Then I would go pick Behrooz up from work in our little old banger. You would have thought

Behrooz would be glad of our improvement in circumstances. But no!

In fact, the jealousy grew as now he did not know where I was at any given time of day. Prior to passing my test and being able to drive myself and the children, we had been housebound, our activities limited to our local area. Now I could take the children to all sorts of places and pastime activities.

Behrooz was so jealous he started taking the mileage of the car before he went to work, saying, "I will know where you have been while I'm out," no matter that I was not doing anything wrong. At first, I thought he was joking; he was not. The control was tightening more and more.

As soon as possible after I had passed my test, Behrooz started taking lessons. Looking back, I realise now, by passing my test, to him, I had undermined his manhood, the twat! Narcissists must have absolute control over everybody and every situation around them. At that point, I had no idea what a narcissist actually was, only that I literally walked on eggshells all day, every day.

A good example of his abuse and control was that no matter what event was going on for the children, or in later years their school events, he would not attend, telling me, "They're your kids; you go," or if there was a problem concerning the children, "They're your kids; you sort it out."

Another good example was when there was a big opening ceremony for a local super DIY store near us taking place at night. Several parents nearby were taking their children to it, as this superstore was pulling out all the stops: a big BBQ and firework display. I tentatively asked Behrooz if we could go, as the children were excited about the firework display. If it had been a daytime event, I would have taken the children without telling Behrooz until after the event, but obviously, because of the planned firework display, it had to be after dark. Behrooz did not like me going out after dark; to his mentality, that's when all affairs and dodgy doings happened. Unbeknownst to Behrooz, I knew for a fact several of the local mothers were all having affairs during daylight hours when their husbands were at work.

Someone I knew told me she was having an affair with the local coal man, and after sex, he would always dust his cap over his todger, coating it with coal dust; otherwise, his Mrs would know he had been unfaithful, as it would have been the only white bit on him when he got home that night. YUK!

Behrooz told me I was lying, as according to him, no store opened with that sort of extravaganza.

"Who was I planning to meet up with?" Again, no trust from him at all. I told him to go ask Mary, who lived just down the road from us, that Mary and her husband Terry were taking their children to the event. The children, although not fully understanding why Behrooz was being adamant that there was no such event happening, started begging their dad to go. Behrooz agreed while telling me he would see if the man I had arranged to meet would be at this event.

On the night of the event, we all turned up at the store. The children were very excited, asking for hot dogs, which I bought for them. Behrooz seemed to be mellow, interacting with his children. To be fair, the crowd that turned up was far larger than I had expected. We were all stood munching hot dogs, waiting for the fireworks display to start, the kids standing in front of Behrooz and myself. Not thinking, I said, "See, I told you I wasn't lying." Behrooz spun on me, shouting, "SHUT YOUR FUCKING MOUTH, YOU FUCKING WHORE!" I felt myself literally crumble inside, actually stooping down from my knees, trying to make myself as small as possible in front of a crowd of hundreds of strangers who were witnessing my humiliation. Thank God the kids were so enthralled by the fireworks display that they did not seem to hear what their dad had just called me in public.

I stood trembling, waiting for the blows to start landing. They did not. I have to thank the crowd of strangers for that. It's like a volcano erupting – once the initial top blows off the volcano, the subsequent lava flow is steadier or stops, pausing for a few days until the pressure builds again.

I suppose, really, it was like being a prisoner of war where the enemy conditions your mind to become their way of thinking. You don't realise what's actually happening to you until it's too late.

Things started increasing in a crescendo of emotional abuse. Behrooz would come home from work talking to me like dirt, calling me really horrible names in front of the children. His favourite was, "YOU UGLY FAT FUCKING CUNTING BASTARD SICK BITCH SEE A PSYCHIATRIST."

I would say, "Please don't call me that; the children are listening." At night in bed, whether I wanted to or not, he would demand sex, taking what he wanted, many times trying to anal rape me and not listening to my pleas to leave me alone. I could not get too loud in my protests in case the children heard and became upset. Subsequently, even with birth control, I became pregnant again, once more suffering horrendously, with morning sickness.

Once I was certain of the pregnancy, I informed Behrooz. He just turned to me, saying, "How?! You were using protection!" My reply was, "Protection is never a hundred percent certain." His reply was, "Well, you better get rid of it then!"

Again, my whole being was devastated. For my husband, the father of my children, to react like this crushed me all over again. But due to my being unable to carry babies without being bedridden for the whole term of a pregnancy and the crippling morning sickness associated with difficult pregnancies, my doctor advised me to have a termination, telling me, "Considering all the hospital investigations you've had, which came back that you should never have been able to have children at all, and the difficulties with the two pregnancies you have had, I will arrange a termination for you." I really did not seem to have a choice.

It was deep winter when the termination happened. Behrooz went off to work as usual that morning, leaving my dad to take me to the hospital and to pick me back up after the procedure.

My mother was minding Aslin and John while I was in the hospital. Upon arriving home, to be fair, my mum made me a cup of tea, asking me if I was okay. A few seconds later, Behrooz walked through the door from work. I looked at him; he just glared at me with a face like thunder, stalking past me, our children, and my parents into the kitchen and into the garden, slamming the back door after himself. We all looked at each other in shock, not knowing what to do for the best. My parents said, "Perhaps it's best if we go and leave you to it; he's possibly upset." As soon as my parents left, Behrooz came in from outside, once again ignoring me and our children, throwing himself into a chair and glowering.

Although I had been told to rest, I got up and made the children some dinner. I did not acknowledge Behrooz or make him anything to eat; I just left the bear alone. I did not poke it.

Once the children were in bed, I asked Behrooz what the hell that was all about. He never even turned his head to look at me or speak to me; it was as if I was invisible. I went up to bed and cried myself to sleep. The next morning, I came downstairs to find Behrooz in exactly the same position. He never spoke a word to me for two weeks after that day. This was the start of his cycle of silences, which preceded violent attacks, but never in front of the children, thank God. In my constant state of terror, I really thought I was protecting my children by not crying out, but now, years later, I know I was wrong. They knew.

Then came the day Behrooz came home from work to find my neighbour Elaine in our lounge having a chat. Usually, Behrooz would put on a front if anyone were in our house, but that day he must have had something happen at work, as he was literally livid when he walked in the door. Seeing Elaine, he erupted, screaming at me in his usual rage, which no one knew about except me, screaming at the neighbour, "What the fuck are you doing in my house? Fuck off to your own house, you cunt!" He then flew across the room at me, flailing into me. Elaine had flown across the road to her husband John, both of them storming back through the front door, which, in all the mayhem, had been left open. All of this took only seconds to happen. Both of my children were screaming, as up to this point, they had never witnessed their dad's treatment of me or his major tirades. John, Elaine's husband, told his wife to go back home and call the police as he stood in front of Behrooz, who, as soon as John had come in my door, had taken a step back from me. Behrooz must have thought John meant for his wife to use our phone to call the police, as Behrooz stepped towards the phone, ripping it from the wall by the cord, which, as he did, propelled the phone across the room, missing our son's head by a millimetre.

That was the catalyst!

The police arrived, the neighbour telling them what he had witnessed, the police asking me if I wanted

Behrooz removed from our property. My reply: yes. My children needed protecting, no matter what my feelings towards my husband.

The police warned Behrooz not to attempt to gain entry to our home, taking him to what, at the time, was a place for single men in the city, The Manor Guild House, situated at the bottom end of Wood End, where he could rent a room.

A couple of days later, Behrooz came knocking on our door, which I was now keeping locked and bolted at all times to prevent access. The children were at school, so out of harm's way. Behrooz seemed really calm, asking me if I would go to the local café with him for tea and to talk. He was abjectly sorry, promising to change, and saying all the usual bullshit men like this use to wheedle their way back into you.

At the café, I made the mistake of sitting in the inside seat of the booth where our tea was being served. As soon as I sat down, I realised I was trapped; an immense wave of panic and terror washed over me. I asked Behrooz to let me out, but he would not. I beckoned the café owner over, asking him to tell my husband to let me out. Thanks be to God, the café owner sized up my predicament. There were a couple of big men sitting nearby having breakfast, and the café owner obviously knew them well.

As soon as the owner said their names, these big lads came to our booth. As is usual for cowards like Behrooz, he moved pretty damn smart away from me, letting me out rather than face these big burly lads. I fled as fast as I could, getting home and locking the doors behind me.

The next day, I went to a solicitor while the children were at school. In those days, there was no waiting for appointments; he saw me straight away. I filled him in, saying I wanted a divorce.

I had not told the children's school anything about our home situation. Now it was a case of trying to find work around the children's school times to provide for them, as I had told my solicitor I did not want anything from Behrooz. He told me whether I did or not, it was law that a father had to provide maintenance for his children, which I couldn't do anything but accept. The amount was set at the minimum of ten pounds a week for each child, nothing for me.

At that point, stupid as I was and naive as I was, I knew on the paltry wage Behrooz got, after paying maintenance for his children and renting a room, he would not have a lot of money left over to feed himself. Again, hindsight is a marvellous thing; I should really have taken the bastard for everything and sod it, but me being me did not.

There now began a period of solicitors' appointments, during which I was informed my husband was throwing accusations against me of having numerous affairs and all sorts of lies.

Then came the day my front door rang, and social services stood on my doorstep. Again, my husband had been to the children's school, telling the headmistress I was neglecting the children and moving strange men into our home. You name the lies; he spouted it to the headmistress, who, to be fair to her, had to act on information received, no matter how wild the accusation was.

Now the so-called professionals were involved, it all became a real nasty period of turmoil, stress, and anxiety. I had now secured four jobs, three of which did not impact the children at all as they all took place while the children were at school, but one was a couple of nights a week working behind a bar at a pub called the Hen and Chickens in the town centre. So, I advertised for a childminder to watch the children when necessary, including the two nights a week I did bar work. Working these four jobs, keeping my home clean and tidy – which I have always prided myself on – and caring for my children took a toll. My weight dropped to just over eight stone, and I was exhausted and worn down, but I still took the children out for fun things to do, be it swimming or to the park. I made damn sure they did not suffer. To be honest, I can't remember them ever asking me if or when their dad would come home!

Social services had arranged for Behrooz and myself, in conjunction with my doctor's records, to have weekly meetings with a psychiatrist. The first meetings were each of us on our own; subsequent ones would be together. I had asked social services why we had to do this, and the reply I got stunned me. Social services were adamant that we should remain together as a family, even though they had documented proof of abuse from Behrooz to me over the years. I asked the social worker, "So, are you telling me that families with addicts, drunkards, and abusers – especially with children – are, in your opinion, better off staying together?" The reply was yes. To this day, I firmly believe social services are a bunch of cretins, and I would not cross the road to piss on a social worker if one were on fire.

You only have to look back over the years at how many poor children have been killed by abusive parents to know I'm dead right about this.

But in those days, with no help from anyone, I was trying my best.

Our psychiatrist sessions continued for a short while. At my last single appointment, the psychiatrist told me he had fears about my husband, saying people like him were the sort who ended up in Broadmoor. All these years later, that psychiatrist was the only one who got it right.

This fell on deaf ears with social services, even after Behrooz turned up at the house one-night ranting that I had sent a solicitor to chase him all over the hospital to serve divorce papers on him. It had nothing to do with me; I did not know that had happened. It turned out Behrooz had moved from the Manor Guild House to a bedsit on Ball Hill, not informing solicitors or me of his move, so they had no option but to serve him at work.

Behrooz, especially as confirmed by the psychiatrist who mentioned the Broadmoor thing about him, is a very plausible man. He can convince anyone of anything – deadly dangerous, like a coiled snake waiting to strike.

As things progressed, he was becoming more and more desperate to get back to the house. He would tell you, if you met him now, that he wanted to get back to his wife and children. Yes, in a way he did, not because he loved us, but because he wanted to be waited on, feted, and served, to have no responsibilities. He was desperate for control; in that moment, he had none.

The childminder I had employed had come recommended, but as I got to know her better, red flags started flying. Her family, it turned out, was well known to the police, her dad being a wife beater.

One night, while I was out working my bar job, she left a pan on the cooker, distracted by a family situation of her own.

I had no alternative but to let both her and my bar job go. Once again, Behrooz tried to use that as a lever with social services to get back into the family. I was having none of it, telling social services I'm not a clairvoyant; I could not foresee the future. As soon as the accident happened, the childminder was gone along with my job, which meant I'm now at home every night with the children.

We were now in a period of some six months from Behrooz being ousted from the house by the police. Things had started to calm a little, with Behrooz being given access to the children every other weekend. He would take them to Birmingham to wander around the Bull Ring shopping centre, the kids coming back with a large bag of pick-and-mix sweets each, which he would tell me he could not afford! So why buy them then? Just tell the kids you can't afford that many; put a limit on what they can have. It's a life lesson, but when you're trying to curry favour with the children you profess to love, it's a way of trying to gain leverage, especially when you're telling social services how great you are by taking your kids to Birmingham for the day.

Behrooz was also trying to get the kids to visit him more often at his bedsit, which they really did not like, so I informed social services of this. They did not like that at all. Back then, social services was a department to be feared, especially when fighting a court case or divorce.

We were now heading up to Christmas. Behrooz was asking when he could see the kids for Christmas. I asked the kids if they would like to go to Daddy's for Christmas Day for a few hours, spending the morning with me for Santa to come, telling them Santa will possibly leave a couple of gifts at their dad's bedsit also. The kids thought it was a great idea – double Santa in one day; who wouldn't at that age?

And social services were pleased we were being amiable for the Christmas period, even though I had stated quite categorically that Behrooz and I would not be getting back together.

So, Christmas Day arrived. The kids had gifts from Santa and a good breakfast with me. I then dropped them off to Behrooz, who was desperately trying to get me to stay along with the kids. I told him this is your time with the kids, what you asked for, not a lever to get me to stay, which is what he was really after; he was using the kids to get to me.

I was supposed to pick them both back up around two hours later. Within those two hours, I had three phone calls from Behrooz telling me the kids wanted me to be there for the food he had made. In the end, I told him, "Right, I'm coming to pick them up now," some thirty minutes earlier than planned. When I got there, the kids were happy to be coming home early, with Behrooz trying to give me food he had prepared to take with us. They did not want the food, saying they were full up. He was less than happy, given the amount of food prepared, proving he had planned all along to try and get me to go to his bedsit with the kids. Instead of looking at the situation as a chance to mend fences, he was using all of us to try and gain control yet again.

After that experience was when I started getting funny phone calls at all hours of the day and night.

I would pick up the phone, say hello, and receive no reply. At first, I thought it had been cut off. Then I started to get the ones with heavy breathing. I thought it was Behrooz playing mind games, but on one occasion, he had actually been at the front door when it happened. He had asked who it was, as the call had made me jittery. I replied, "Wish I knew; it's been happening a bit lately."

Then someone started following me home, first in a car, which, at first, I thought must have been someone looking for an address in our road. Then I started to see a shady figure loitering about the street in the dark, wearing a parka. By now, I was becoming terrified. I rang the police, who basically did not want to know, telling me I was imagining it. The kids had told Behrooz all about it. He couldn't have been nicer, telling me, "Let me come back home; I will protect you all. I'm a changed man."

This was in conjunction with the psychiatrist telling Behrooz he must attend anger management, which he had agreed to but was waiting for dates.

At that point, I really did not know if I was coming or going. Mentally, I felt like I was made of glass that had cracks all over it; if someone touched the glass, it would shatter into a million pieces. Then social services dropped a bombshell on me, telling me if I did not get back with Behrooz, they would take the kids away and put them in a home. When I said to them, "You can't do that; you have no grounds," they told me to watch them, claiming the courts will always take children away from one-parent families. I asked, "What, even if one parent is a nut job or an addict or abuser?" They said, "The courts always act on our recommendations." I was terrified and in turmoil.

Now bear in mind, in those days in the early eighties, social services were the be-all and end-all. I was of the generation that had been brought up being told by my parents, "If you don't behave, social services will put you in a home; you will never see us again." I was terrified but determined, until that weekend when a young couple I knew through one of my jobs invited me and the kids to their house for a bit of a kids' party. It was fabulous; the kids were so excited, and it gave me a bit of time to sit and relax, enjoying my kids enjoying themselves. However, when we got back home, not long after, we found that the house had been burgled and ransacked. Taking all my jewellery and the club money out of the cupboard for the catalogue I ran. The police were called; all they did was take a few notes, telling me there was nothing much they could do, that I should inform my insurance company and make lists of what was missing. Now, with all the turmoil going on around me, this on top was the final straw.

The police rang Behrooz, telling him about the robbery. The kids were upset, obviously knowing strangers had been in our home. Behrooz arrived while the police were there, telling them he would comfort the kids and talk to me. The kids were pleased to see their dad under the circumstances.

I was in a right old state, what with social services decreeing they would be putting the kids in a home, the robbery, and the stalker. I just accepted Behrooz being back in the house, with him telling me in front of the police, "It's okay; go to bed, rest. I will stay up all night in this chair and keep you all safe," which he did.

The next morning, after the kids went to school, he sat very rationally and talked to me very much like he used to before we were married, assuring me that if we got back together, which he very much wanted, he would go to anger management help and do more with the kids. I could do whatever job I wanted – all very sane, very plausible.

I agreed, and over the next two days, he moved back in. We, however, slept in separate rooms for six months, as even though he sounded sane and plausible, as my mother said, "Leopards do not change their spots." During those six months, the insurance claim went through for the robbery.

There was mention of it taking a while for the anger management course to come through, but as it was all calm, to me it was all plausible, natural progression. Social services had buggered off, knowing all the details about us getting back together. Solicitors had been told the divorce was no longer happening; things seemed to be going along very well.

It was just after the insurance came through from the break-in that Behrooz turned up at home with my jewellery taken in the robbery. I asked him what the hell, how have you got that, his reply I did the break-in, I needed a lever to make you realise how vulnerable you were without me and how much you needed me.

It worked, did it not!

OMG!

He really was a raving maniac, and I was stuck.

The letter from the anger management course dropped on the doormat a little while after our six-month reunion, Behrooz calmly telling me he would take time off work to go. That night was the first time since reuniting that we slept together. Behrooz went off to work the next morning, and I sorted the kids out, coming back home from school. The phone was ringing; it was the anger management course saying they had a cancellation and would my husband like it. I explained he was at work but would get him to ring them back when he got home. Behrooz duly arrived back home, and I imparted the information to him.

Behrooz said, "No, I'm not going. I don't need anger management; things have been going along okay, haven't they? Recently I told you I'm a changed man. You ring them, tell them I'm not going, and that you're happy with things the way they are now."

Alarm bells rang in my brain!

My reply to Behrooz was, "I'm not happy. You promised you would take this course. If you're determined not to go, things had better not change, and you ring them to cancel. I sure as hell am not."

I left him to it; he rang and cancelled the course. I could not make him attend. For about a month, things carried on as they were, then slowly started to disintegrate, but done so surreptitiously. You don't realise you are being controlled again. Things like asking me, "Where are you going today? What are you doing? Who with? What time?" and so on. Then when he got home, quizzing me several times, asking the same questions in different formats. When you are a mother dealing with children, a job, and all the other everyday things in your life, you just don't realise exactly how much control is being applied to you as you are constantly distracted by your life around you.

CHAPTER 12

One day, I had taken the kids into town just for a look-see. We had a snack and wandered around the Herbert Art Gallery. On the way back to the car park, I had purchased a new handbag from a shop called Salisbury's that used to be in Broadgate. That's all they sold: their suitcases, handbags, etc.

I will always remember that blue clutch handbag, not because it was anything fancy, but because it was a weapon Behrooz used to remind me just what control looked like. Upon arriving back home, I had put the receipt for the handbag on the mantel shelf above the fire, thinking nothing of it.

When Behrooz came home that night, it was the usual, "What have you done today? Who with?" My automated replies about mine and the kids' day out met his gaze. He looked at me in a really funny way

– not unusual, I thought nothing of it – until the next day after taking the kids to school, when I got back to the house and found Behrooz holding the receipt in his hand. As soon as I walked through the door, he pounced, grabbing me by the arm, dragging me across the lounge, shoving the handbag receipt into my face, screaming, "You fucking whore! Why are you lying to me again?" Shocked, stunned, horrified, I struggled free, saying, "What the hell!"

Now what's set you off? He was screaming at me, "You have been to Salisbury with some bloke. Here's the bill for your hotel room where you have been fucking, and I don't suppose you know what disc and wonkin is either?"

Um! Actually, no, I don't. I have no idea what the hell you're on about. He threw the bill at me. I caught it, looking at it. To this day, I still, some thirty-odd years later, cannot get over that tirade; it's etched indelibly on my memory.

I looked at that bill, flustered, thinking, "God, he really is mad; he really has lost the plot." I picked up my blue clutch handbag, saying, "Well, if you think this is the bill for a hotel room, it was really cheap. This is the handbag I bought from Salisbury's in Broadgate when I took the kids into town the other day. If you don't believe me, ask the kids when they come home." He continued to scream about disc and wonkin! Once again, I looked at the receipt, where printed were the words disc and wonkin, some sort of computer language used by Sailsbury's to track their stock.

I shouted back, "You're a raving bloody lunatic! Of course, I don't know what disc and wonkin means. Ring the bloody shop, or better still, get in the bloody car now. We will go to the shop; they can explain to a raving lunatic what their business terminology means!" That stopped him dead, and to be honest, it surprised me. I expected an escalation as I was answering back, a thing I had never done before, but by now, I had enough of this senseless tirade of anger and manipulation. He just turned on his heel and stormed out the door to work.

From previous experience and spending the day on tenterhooks awaiting a cascade of tyranny when he arrived back home from work, my nerves were frayed, only to be surprised again when he did get back home that he was as near to normal as could be for him.

Another ploy the next day was the start of the silences.

At first, I was pleased, thinking again it was another new phase and that he was regretting his actions and that we had turned a corner, until I realised every question I asked, every conversation I tried to start, was met with stony silence. The kids were asking, "What's wrong with Dad?" My reply was, "He's in a bad mood and sulking," which he was, the knob.

Even the kids never had tantrums, especially epic ones like Behrooz had. As the days wore on, the stress was unimaginable, trying to be normal for the kids while walking on eggshells around the Knobhead. Eventually, the silence broke with an almighty bang – literally. He slammed into the house from the back garden. I was washing up dishes in the sink when he flew across the kitchen, grabbing me and shaking me until my teeth rattled, screaming at me that I was a fat, ugly, fucking, cunting bastard sick bitch who should see a psychiatrist. Apparently, the boss of his department had taken him to task over his handling of a patient at work, giving him a warning. Behrooz blamed me, saying it was because he couldn't trust me; his brain was constantly worrying about what I was getting up to at home while he was at work.

No matter what I said, it made no difference. He then proceeded to tell me we must move, as all the neighbours were talking about him. That bit was quite possible, as when he started, I was surprised if the people in the next town over couldn't hear his ranting. And since his extreme behaviour had escalated, the neighbours were avoiding me. I was becoming increasingly isolated both at home and outside; the only time I could breathe was while at work.

Things calmed down a bit, Behrooz becoming calm after this vent. Even though he had shaken me badly, I had no visible bruises at that point.

My mother always used to tell me a ditty:

> *"Sticks and stones may break your bones, but words will never hurt you."*

She was dead wrong about that.

To this day, I wake sometimes in the night with Behrooz saying, "You fat, ugly, fucking, cunting bastard sick bitch, see a psychiatrist," ringing in my ears.

Over the next few days, we talked, and I thought moving would be a fresh start for us all. With no one to turn to for help, I was stuck, so maybe the move of house would be the solution to Behrooz's behavioural issues.

CHAPTER 13

We started to look for properties, eventually settling on an ex-council property in Black Watch Road, Coventry, a nice three-bedroom place with a large garden backing onto the old aerodrome, which was now a sports field and club. Lots of space for the kids to run around the garden, which I thought would keep Behrooz occupied in his downtime. The school was literally ten houses away from our place, and a shopping centre, doctor's, library, and dentist were all just around the corner, with a secondary school, Barr's Hill, about a fifteen-minute walking distance away for when the kids started secondary school.

On the day of the move, the furniture van arrived. It had been organised with the movers that they would give Behrooz a lift to the new house once the van was packed, while I went to pick up the keys for the new house, taking the kids with me to tidy before the van and Behrooz arrived at the new place.

As soon as the van arrived, I departed, picked up the keys, and went to the new house, cleaning, and sorting. The kids were exploring and having a fine time in their new garden. The van arrived from the old house. "No Behrooz?" I asked the guys. "Where is my husband? You were supposed to be giving him a lift over." They had no idea, saying he was nowhere around when we left. I jumped in the car with the kids, leaving the guys to start unloading, going back to the old house to find Behrooz – no sign of him. I made my way back along the route from the old to the new house, finding him coming out of a public phone box right outside the kids' old school. He was raging, saying, "You fucking bitch! Leaving me at the old house." My reply: "For fuck's sake, what's wrong with you? The guys couldn't see you when ready to leave. What were you doing? It's your fault, not mine! I cannot be in two places at the same time. And why didn't you ring me from the old house to tell me you were still there instead of wandering around the streets? It's your fault, not mine! Get in the bloody car." There was no way he would have gotten physical, as it was broad daylight in the middle of a public street. But what he did do was sulk all the way back to the new house – not a good omen for the future. Upon arrival at the new house, it was like a switch had been flicked; upon seeing the moving guys, there were no repercussions for them, just camaraderie and niceness.

What a two-faced knobhead. I totally ignored him, getting on with sorting stuff out into the new house. I couldn't find all my pans prior to leaving the old house; I had left Behrooz to pack these last few items, having used them the night before moving to cook a meal. God knows what he had been doing after I left the old house that morning. It turned out they were still in the cupboards at the old house, which once again I had to go back to and box them up to bring over to the new house, leaving Behrooz while I did that to do what he did best: stand doing fuck all while sulking in the new house, supposedly overseeing the guys finish depositing our belongings from the moving van.

Me, being the idiot I was, thought, "It's all the stress of moving; it will all be fine once we are settled."

It really was not. It had been a really long day. We left some of the boxes for the next day, going up to bed. I was exhausted; I was just dropping off to sleep when the front door started going. It must have been about midnight. Behrooz went down to answer it; it was one of the movers, saying he had lost his bank book and if we found it, could we contact him? I could hear Behrooz ranting, telling this guy, "You could have waited till tomorrow." In this situation, Behrooz was right. He came back upstairs, telling me, "Have you slept with that man?" For fuck's sake, so much for a new start. I just told Behrooz, "Don't even go there. So much for new beginnings, you knob head. I'm not even going to dignify that with a reply."

The next morning, we were still sorting moving boxes, putting our new house to rights when Aslin came to her dad with a bank book in her hand, saying it was in one of my boxes. "Dad, it's not yours or Mum's name inside it; it was the moving man's book. It must have fallen from his top pocket into my box while being moved." I just glared at Behrooz, wanting nothing to do with him or the book. He said, "Ring the company, tell them we have found the bank book." My reply was, "Do it yourself. If you think I'm having anything to do with the book or that man, you're wrong. After what you said to me last night, you idiot, do you really think I'm going to give you any ammunition to fire at me? So much for false promises, Behrooz." I was shocked as he actually looked shamefaced for once. He never argued, just picked up the phone and rang the company to explain. When the chap duly arrived later that night to pick his book up, I would not answer the door. I just sat watching Behrooz until he rose to open the door, making it quite clear by my stance – not moving – that I was less than impressed by my husband's behaviour; it seemed that even with a house move, nothing had changed, and I was expecting him to honour his word on being a changed man. Thus far, there was no sign he was.

Once established in the new house, things settled down. The kids were settled in their new school, and John had come on leaps and bounds in reading, over which I was thrilled.

Behrooz had changed his job role at work, which entailed different shifts, giving me and the kids much more freedom from his ominous foreboding presence. And a week every six weeks of night shifts. Boy, did I enjoy those night shifts – a whole bed to myself, nobody thrashing about next to me pulling the covers off me all night, and definitely no perverted sexual demands, which I constantly refused. Such refusals always led to sleepless nights for me as my inner alarms were triggered. In the past, on occasions, I had to literally fight Behrooz off to avoid being raped in various ways, usually when it got loud. That stopped him, wary of the kids arriving in the bedroom to see what all the ruckus was about.

Remember, these were the eighties when spousal abuse was a known thing – not taken as a crime like it is these days – and no help from anyone, as told to me by those so-called professionals when I had left him. "Stay with your abuser; it's what they considered best. Or they take your kids and put them in a home." That was the axe they held over your heads in those days. They should all be ashamed of the way things were then.

Recently, I met a lady who suffered the same as I did. She told me that the very same thing happened to her; the only difference was that her parents backed her up when it got to the point of leaving her husband, even going as far as to buy her a house so she could be free. I had nothing like that to help me.

And so, I carried on. It helped, or so I once again thought, that the job I had been doing looked as if it was coming to an end. I had been the manager of a crew of mainly women staff across the country doing promotional work and merchandising for an agency in Sheffield. This agency was going bankrupt. I later found out that the office manager there was siphoning money out of the business. No wonder she could afford her own racehorse and wore designer clothes, all obtained fraudulently with the cash she had stolen from the agency. The job had been really interesting. I enjoyed driving about the UK, visiting myriad different venues, pushing products that would be advertised on television to the public, then merchandising them into vastly different shops and stores across the UK.

There had been times when I had to meet male workers to handle certain venues and products that were far too heavy for my female staff to manage. I never told Behrooz about those times, as it would lead to the usual "you're shagging these men" rants. There was one occasion when I was held up on the way home at Spaghetti Junction, which had only just recently opened, by a huge lorry fire. The M6 was backed up for miles. Usually, if I were going to be late, I would ring home to tell Behrooz, but there was no way of doing that from Spaghetti Junction, which is so high up in the air that there is no access to the ground. Back then, there were no mobile phones. When I eventually got home, Behrooz was sitting in the lounge with such a look on his face that I immediately thought something had happened. I asked, "What's wrong?" before realising it was another case of "She's out shagging again while I'm the poor put-upon husband living with a whore". He wouldn't even look at me or speak to me. The kids were running about playing, so he couldn't show his true colours and give me a slap like he would have if they had not been home. Then John turned on the television as I was explaining about the lorry fire on the M6, with Behrooz continuing to sneer at me and give me the look that said I was in for it later, as he did not believe a word I was saying. When the news came on, lo and behold, there was an aerial view of the M6, the lorry fire, and the traffic tailed back for miles. I spun on my heel, pointing at the news item, saying, "There you go," thinking, "My God, that's a blessing from God; it will all be all right now." Once again, I was wrong. As soon as the kids were asleep that night, I got yet another slap for making him worry – not about my safety, but because he thought I had been shagging again, as I am a whore.

While Behrooz's new job role brought in extra money, it was still a struggle on just one wage, especially around the time of moving. Maggie Thatcher had come into power, and every household in the UK was suffering from a rise in costs due to her inept management of the UK economy, which continued for an eleven-year period.

In the old days, after the war, women went to work for what was termed "pin money". Their husbands kept the wages they earned, giving their wives just enough to keep the wolf from the door, not leaving anything for wives to spend on themselves. But in the eighties, wives went to work to contribute to the household expenses, and it still remains that way today in most households.

So, coupled with my agency going bankrupt and the work from there drying up, along with Behrooz's constant distrust of me – "Where have you been? Who with? Which man are you shagging today?" – it was time for a change. The house move sure had not worked, along with his promises of changing.

I sat and wrote to every large supermarket chain in Coventry, explaining my knowledge of promotions and products and asking if they had any vacancies and if one of them would give me a job. The wage would be far less than my last job, but the hours would be stable, giving Behrooz far less opportunity to distrust me; I would be in the same place, day in and day out, on a stable shift pattern. Abuse is very insidious, creeping along; you just don't realise you are being abused.

It takes years for a controlled abused person to realise that no matter what they do, the abuser will never stop, so at this point, I was still in the "If I do this or if I do that, Behrooz will realise and stop" scenario.

One supermarket, Tesco, at Dorchester Way, Coventry, came back to me with a job interview – handy, really, as it is literally only a quarter of a mile from Behrooz's workplace, Walsgrave Hospital, so we could most days travel to work and back together.

The interview went well; they offered me a job on the spot, but only as a general assistant in the home and wear department, which I accepted, starting on the second of January 1990.

The work was menial, filling and cleaning the home and wear department. The hours were stable, the pay really poor, and for those of you reading this story, if you have read my first book, *Sex, Drugs, Bread Rolls, and Armed Robberies*, you will know what a den of iniquity Tesco is and what happened to me while working there.

Most days, Behrooz and I would travel to work together, dependent on shift hours. Either he would have control of the car, or I would. If I finished before him, usually I would go straight home, doing housework and cooking a meal before going back to pick him up from the hospital. The kids were attending school, transitioning from primary to secondary, both with good grades. However, in all their school lives, Behrooz would not attend a single event that the school held, telling me, "They're your kids; you go, I'm busy." I never ever missed one single event. John in particular was crushed when he came first in science, the science teacher pulling him outside in the playground, saying, "You, boy, come here." John told me the thought was, "Blimey, what have I done wrong?" But when John got to the teacher, he was told, "Do you realise what you have done?" John, befuddled, said, "No, sir, I do not." The teacher then patted him on the back, saying, "Well done! In all my years as a teacher, it's the first time a pupil has ever got 100% in the science exam. You have made it tough for me, as now I will have to sit and devise a totally new exam for pupils going forward."

I was thrilled; so much so, I took John to town on my next day off, buying him a pair of trainers he had always wanted. What did his piece of shit dad do? Nothing, just looked at his son saying, "Okay, so next time, do the exam this way or that way." I stood in front of Behrooz, saying, "You could at least tell your son well done. No good telling him to do the exam this or that way; the exam is now defunct, useless – your son has trashed it. And if his teacher can heap praise on your son, why can't you?" He just sneered, turning on his heel and walking away. The bastard.

I can honestly say the only thing that man ever bought his kids was when Aslin needed new shoes. Behrooz was trying to get her to wear men's shoes, saying they would last longer. I was having none of that. We went to town to the shop to be seen buying shoes from Dolcis in the precinct, where Aslin picked out a pair of good, strong women's shoes costing forty pounds. Behrooz showed himself up, saying he wasn't going to pay for them as they wouldn't last long. I told him, "Right, you pay for the bloody left foot; I will pay for the bloody right foot." The cashier was looking at Behrooz like he was something that had crawled from under a stone, which he was. Aslin was delighted with her shoes, and they lasted that child two years before they fell apart.

At home, once again things settled. Even though Behrooz was now able to find me at any time at work, at home the physical, emotional, and sexual abuse continued.

The silences were the worst; I never knew just when the Cobra would strike, usually at the most unexpected moments. Behrooz continued to work overtime, coming home, eating his meal, and promptly falling asleep in front of the fire instead of interacting with his children. He continued to tell me the kids were all my responsibility. To be honest, if I had been a single parent, things would have been far easier; we were all held back by that man. Too late for me, but Aslin is doing a mature student's degree at university. Once that is done, she then wants to do a master's. Fair play to her – you go, girl! John has been less lucky, as those reading my first book will know, but he's getting there.

Behrooz continued to control every aspect of our lives. The only one time I persuaded him to come swimming with us as a family, we all arrived at the baths – John and Behrooz going off into the men's changing rooms, Aslin and I to the ladies'. Aslin and I were in the water; we waited and waited – no sign of Behrooz and John. Then I saw them both on the spectators' balcony, Behrooz with a face like thunder, John very upset. I called to Aslin, saying something is wrong; let's get out of the water. I stood under Behrooz, calling up to him, "What's wrong?" No reply: he just glared at me, turning his back on me. I asked John, "What's wrong, son?" He peered up at his dad fearfully, saying nothing. I told John, "Okay, I'm coming, won't be long." Taking Aslin, we went to the changing rooms. Once dry and clothed, we went to find Behrooz and John, who by this time had made their way downstairs to the foyer. Upon arriving, I asked Behrooz again, "What's wrong?" He rounded on me, calling me a fucking bitch, saying, "You didn't tell me I needed a pound coin for a locker in the men's changing rooms." As the women's changing rooms' lockers were free, it never occurred to me that the men's wouldn't be the same. I thought, "Bugger this." I rounded back on Behrooz, saying, "Well, as I've never been in the men's changing rooms, how would I know you needed a pound coin? And what was wrong with asking the attendant to get you one? This is just an excuse once again not to interact with your wife and children." He was staggered; I was in a public place – no room for his fists here. He stalked off, shouting he was going home. Sadly, we had to follow; he had the car and house keys, and I had no money for the bus. It was a long, arduous walk from town to home; I could do it, but not the kids. If we had not gone, he would have left us stranded. The only good thing was when we got home, he went to bed. I really hoped he would never wake up.

The kids were upset, but I managed to make light of the situation, cheering them up and distracting them. Poor little mites.

Behrooz by now was coming home telling me all about this chap (Anton) he worked with who was never at his home, never interacted with his kids, and how Anton's kids were going off the rails, having police involvement around his kids and the trouble they were in. I couldn't believe Behrooz did not realise he was doing exactly the same thing with our kids. He was never at home, and when he was, he never interacted with the kids, never attended any of their school events, nothing. I told Behrooz point blank, "You're exactly the same. The difference between Anton and us is me. I am the one steering our children through life", whereas Anton's wife, whom I had met, was the same as Anton and Behrooz. She couldn't give a monkey's what her kids got up to. Behrooz was damn lucky our kids were more grounded. Aslin was always getting into trouble at school; she's like me, has a big gob, and vocalises her thoughts, whereas John was so quiet you would never know he was there.

Then came the day Aslin backchatted her teacher, who told her he was going to ring home and speak to her dad. Aslin said, "Do not ring home; my dad is on nights, he will be asleep, and my mum's at work."

I can laugh about it now, but at the time it was horrendous. This teacher took no notice of Aslin and rang home. Behrooz answered the phone, and being woken up, was raging. He did no more than fly up to the school threatening the teacher with all sorts, then came home to ring me at work. Our receptionist put his call through to me, saying, "Your husband's on the phone; brace yourself." So, God knows what he must have said to her before she put him through to me. He was incandescent, ranting and raging, calling me all the usual things, telling me, "They're your kids; you should have sorted this out." When I could get a word in, I told Behrooz, "Well, if I had known about a problem with Aslin at school, as usual, you won't have anything to do with the kids and school, I possibly would have ended up sorting the problem out. But to be quite honest, it's about time you manned up and became an actual dad. It won't hurt you to be a parent for once." Oh my God, if the filth he was spewing before I said that was bad, you should have heard what came next. I just put the phone down on him, finding myself shaking like a leaf.

It was with great trepidation that at the end of my workday, I made my way home, getting there before the kids arrived home from school in case of another vile tirade against them from Behrooz. But no, nothing was said to them, thank goodness, just the usual rant at me.

The next day, a letter arrived at our house from the headmaster of Aslin's school, stating that on this occasion, the school would take no legal action against Behrooz. However, Behrooz was banned from Aslin's school for life; if he ever set foot on school grounds again, he would be arrested.

I showed Behrooz the letter, and he went crazy at me. I stood my ground, telling him he had shown his true colours now, so he better watch himself. But what the school had done by sending that letter compounded Behrooz's lack of interest and any possibility of him ever attending his children's school in the future when they won awards.

The effect this escapade had was that now Behrooz knew he had shown himself up, so he had to be more circumspect at home. The kids were now nearing the end of their school days. Aslin was going to college, which she did try but found the curriculum not to her liking. Aslin then spent many years doing various other jobs before leaving home at age twenty-five to move to Yorkshire to live with a man she met on an internet dating site who was twenty years older than her. To me, what Aslin was doing then was trying to get in her relationship the proper father figure she never got in her childhood. The relationship lasted five years before Aslin came back to Coventry, where she worked with Axa before they closed down. Axa offered Aslin a position in their Bristol branch, but she did not want to move there. It was around this time that she got pregnant with my youngest grandchild, having Arden at age thirty-six.

CHAPTER 14

John was by now in a group of Asian friends, going out and about with them, which I did not think was a bad thing. I was wrong; one of them had been a friend all through his school days.

John was working on a Saturday at my Tesco store in Jubilee Crescent, Coventry, literally just up the road from our house. After leaving school, he attended college. Being really artistic, he had said he wanted to do a graphic design course, which I was thrilled about. His course hours had some large gaps in them, so he asked if he could pick up extra hours at Tesco, which the store manager agreed to. I, in my naïveté, thought this was a good idea as he seemed to have a good work ethic. Little did I know that a combination of his group of Asian friends and an older woman working at Tesco would be the downfall of my son.

Then Behrooz had an accident at work that caused a back problem he already had, giving him an excuse to stay off work for over a year, which was pure hell for me. While he had been at work, his temper and abuse had been somewhat manageable in a certain way; now I was faced with the cobra twenty-four-seven. Aslin was gone, living in Yorkshire, so she did not suffer. John was either at work, or so I thought, or at college.

Behrooz's abuse increased tenfold. Again, if any of you reading this has seen the film 'Sleeping with the Enemy', you will get a glimpse of my life.

Behrooz would sit in the lounge not speaking for weeks at a time, which was overpowering in itself. The deathly silences were like a black cloud of doom hanging over you, as you never knew when the Cobra would strike. Or he would be ranting through the window at people walking past, such as, "Look at that Irish cunt! What's he doing?" or "That Black bastard is walking past our house. Do you know him? Have you slept with him? Does he know I'm in the house?". Who the hell knew if the man walking past was Irish or, yes, the man was Black, but was he a good man or not? It was not my place to cast aspersions on people just walking past my home.

If I did not answer quickly enough, a slap would land, or an object would be thrown, or I would be pounced on for sex, which by now, thanks to his bad back, was non-existent. Thank God the other bonus to his bad back was that when he pounced, I could get away easily. Oftentimes, I would be left hurt and bleeding on the floor while he walked away, leaving me there, telling me there's no love left for me, is there, Chris? No, there sure as shit is not. The only reason I was still there was that my son was still living in the house.

John was starting to miss college, giving one excuse after another. He was rarely at home; at work, he was doing his job, then started taking on more hours. I tried to talk to him; he eventually said he did not want to be at college anymore, that he wanted to take a gap year, continuing to work at my Tesco store, where the manager had offered John a trainee manager position. When kids are in their difficult teenage years, it's so hard to be able to advise them. At the end of the day, it's their life. So, John gave up college, taking a full-time position at Tesco but turning down the offered management role. Again, it's his life; you have to give them breathing space.

Then came the night the police brought John home. He had been stopped and searched, the police finding a small bit of weed on him. I was mortified. The officer who brought John home told us "it's a first offence. I have not done anything about it but advised him not to be a silly boy as he is a stand-up kind of lad". As he was saying this, Behrooz launched himself at John, punching him in the face. I don't know who was more shocked out of us all. The policeman grabbed Behrooz, saying, "Right, that's bang out of order. He's your son; talk to him. This behaviour is wrong. You are pushing your son away; he needs a dad, not abuse. You're lucky I'm not arresting you for assault." John had fled out of the house at this point. In front of the policeman, I told Behrooz, "You're nothing but shit. Just when you're supposed to be a man, you're a coward. John needs guidance at this point, not violence." The police officer said to me, "I will leave you to it, love. You have my sympathy." Behrooz, as soon as the door was shut behind the officer, started ranting at me with the "your kids" routine. I gave back as good as I got, telling him he had never been a dad and only just a provider. I had been the main breadwinner all our lives and the only parent. Why didn't he just fuck off and leave? "You have never thought of us as our family; to you, your family is the one you left in Iran." John didn't return for two days; I was frantic.

A couple of days later, John came home. I asked him where he had been. He said, "I have a girlfriend; I stayed with her." Shocked again, his dad was asking him who she was. John said, "It's nothing to do with you, Dad."

Can't blame him for that.

The next day at work, I walked into the staff restaurant to find John cuddling a woman called Emma. This woman is known in my first book as Mrs Rare. I was stunned; there was no one else in the staff restaurant, so I confronted them. It turned out Emma had been seeing my son for some eighteen months, both inside and outside of work. Emma was in a relationship with a man to whom she was engaged and had a child with.

The worst thing was every single person who worked there knew, and not one solitary person was kind enough to tip me the wink about the pair of them.

There then followed a period of me trying to talk to John to tell him just what I knew about Emma: all her affairs, her getting a manager the sack by accusing him of sexual misconduct when it was just a ruse to get back at this manager for not leaving his wife to be with her, the sexual liaison she had with the first aider running the course I had sent her on, the Securicor chap at the back door in what was supposed to be a secure van, the young girl on checkouts who had been invited to Emma's house only to flee after being approached for a threesome by Emma and her chap – the list went on. John was a fool in love. Emma had woven her web very tightly; after eighteen months, he believed everything she told him. Being a softy and a gentle giant, he believed he was protecting her from what she had told John was an abusive relationship. We at Tesco knew from her past history there was no abuse. The only reason she was not married to the father of her daughter was that just before their marriage, Emma had confessed to her chap all the affairs she had had while with him, telling him she wanted to start the marriage with a clean slate. His mother, whom I later became friends with, told me her son had been devastated, telling his mum he couldn't marry Emma now because he couldn't trust her. But for the sake of their child, he would stay with her.

By now, I was at an all-time low mentally, emotionally, and physically. My strength was exhausted. A lifeline was thrown to me by a friend at work, Mable. She had lost her husband, Cedric, some months earlier very suddenly. I had adored her husband – such a salt-of-the-earth kind of man who reminded me so much of my own dad.

Mable had booked a holiday in Gran Canaria. It was her practice to holiday once a year with her youngest son's mother-in-law. On this occasion, the mother-in-law was poorly and had been told she could not fly, so Mable offered me the holiday at a discounted rate. I went home telling Behrooz, like it or lump it, I'm going on this holiday. He was furious, but at that point, I knew if I did not get a break, I would actually break. John was okay with me not being there for a week; he said, "I won't be at home much anyway, Mum. I will stay with my friends."

So, Mable and I flew off. Now, I knew Mable had, since her husband's passing, been flirting with the security guard at work and had had a liaison with a chap she had met while on a night out, which to be fair had shocked me. But as Mable said, her husband had not been able to have sex with her for some eight years prior to his passing. As she termed it, "for the last eight years I have lived like a nun. Cedric and I had always said whichever one of us went first, the other one must carry on living".

All well and good, but bloody hell, what happened to grieving? Her poor husband really was not cold in his grave, and she had started chasing men.

Her behaviour had shocked me, but boy was I in for some real eye-opening behaviour on that holiday. We arrived at the hotel and settled in, making our way to the pool. Beside the pool was a bar manned by three staff, all males. At four o'clock daily, they had happy hour: two drinks for the price of one. Mable and I would take turns going up to buy our drinks. As Mable returned from the bar, she said Michael, one of the bartenders, had asked her on a date. None of my business. She proceeded to say, "I'm just going down to the room, stay here, do not come to the room." There's me thinking, "odd".

But hey ho!

Then I realised Michael, who had been collecting glasses around the pool, was watching as Mable walked towards our room. Seeing her enter the room, he dumped all the glasses he had in his hands on a table and followed Mable into our room. Light bulb moment and shock; as I said, none of my business. About thirty minutes later, as I sat reading my book by the pool, a shadow came over me. Startled, I looked up. It was Mable. She said, "Don't you look at me like that."

Startled, I said, "What are you on about? Your shadow startled me." The look on her face was hard. She then proceeded to tell me Michael and she had just had sex in our room, and she was surprised the walls in our room were still standing, that Michael was all man, and she would no longer be living like a nun. Hence the change in her bikini from the one she had on as she had gone into our room to the one she had on coming out of our room. My reply: "Mable, what you do is your business; however, I really hope you used protection, as if Michael is doing that with you, how many other women has he done that with in just this week alone?" She was not a bit frazzled.

So much for a date; it was actually just pure shagging, which happened twice more during that week.

One night, just before we were due to come back home, Mable told me, "Don't come down to the room; Michael is coming down to me." I was not bothered; I had said my piece to her, if she wanted to take VD home with her. I sat with a few people we had made friends with while at the hotel, drinking and chatting, when I saw the pool bar close down and Michael and the other staff walking towards the exit, passing us by as they went. I said to Michael, "Aren't you going the wrong way? Mable is waiting for you in our room." The cheeky swine said, "No, tonight it is your turn." As he approached me, I put my hand up, palm out, saying, "Stop right there; I'm a married woman." His reply: "It does not matter." My reply: "It does to me." Okay, my marriage was pure shit, but I have always been faithful, and I couldn't believe the audacity of the man.

He just laughed and carried on walking, leaving the complex and Mable waiting in our room. About an hour later, Mable came back up to the table. I told her Michael's gone home; she never replied, just got a drink, and sat down chatting, but I could see she was a little bit off – hurt feelings – but as Michael was obviously a lothario, what did she expect? I never ever told her Michael had propositioned me as he went past, why rub salt in her wounds?

Mable had also told me she had invited Michael to visit her in the UK, to which he had agreed. That never happened; it was all a ploy – something which these lotharios said to the women they were shagging to get what they wanted. Not only did Michael obtain sex with Mable, but a good bit of money as well. On the day after he had left her waiting in our room, she had a bag of money in her hand – not just change but notes as well. Innocently, I asked her what it was for, thinking maybe she was going to buy something while we were out for the day, as it would have been heavy to carry.

Mable said, "It's for Michael; he collects foreign money." I just looked at her, thinking, I bloody bet he does – payment for services rendered and then some. There must have been over a hundred pounds in that bag. To me, it was pathetic; after being left waiting by this lothario, to then go and give this lothario a bag of money really smacked of desperation, especially as I had watched Michael just prior to Mable giving him that money do exactly the same as he had done with Mable – follow another woman into her room after dumping a bundle of glasses he had been collecting on a table. To this day, I cannot get over the way Mable comported herself on that holiday while making out to the whole world she was a grieving, respectable widow who was always so stuffy, well-dressed, a cut above everyone else, while honestly, she was, in actual fact, a tart.

That night, Mable and I went for a walk along the sea front, passing by a bandstand where they were playing music, singing, and dancing. I'm chatting away to Mable when I realised, she had disappeared. I turned back to look for her, couldn't see her anywhere, then spotted her in a crushing embrace against the back of the bandstand wall with some chap!

Oh my God, my knee-jerk reaction was, so now who's the lothario here (Mable)? It seemed she certainly wasn't fussy, for sure. If Behrooz knew what had gone on with Mable on that holiday, he would have killed me, thinking if Mable's doing that, so is my wife, as obviously according to Behrooz, I do not have a brain of my own or any morals at all.

That holiday was all a pure revelation to me.

Once back in England, I returned to work. Things at home were pretty much the same as when I had left, but now I was more resolute in my dealings with Behrooz.

John was carrying on seeing Emma, who was still living with the father of her child. Mable was still trawling the store customers and our area for her next lothario, asking me to now accompany her on nights out. To my horror, I started going, thinking, "fuck you, Behrooz".

Watching Mable flirt her way around the local men while keeping myself to myself, I can say Mable actually took home, to my knowledge, during those nights out and had short relationships with, four other local men. One she actually moved into her home for a short period, and one she moved into his home with for a short period, that one buying her white gold jewellery and taking her on holidays to America, where he had family. None of them lasted.

Behrooz was getting more and more deranged but now realising his hold over me was diminishing. I had started looking for a property I could rent with a view to leaving him.

When John got a late-night call from Emma, it catapulted us all into a very serious situation.

Somehow, Emma's partner had found out about her relationship with John and had thrown her out of their house. Emma had rung John, who immediately went to her, obtaining a place to stay with Emma from one of his mates for a few days.

This was when John left home, realistically. He stayed with Emma at this rental for a couple of days while Emma tried to sort out the situation with her partner and her child.

It was a very tense time all around, both at work and home. Emma's child was sent to stay with her paternal grandparents, who subsequently later on obtained a court residence order for the child to stay with them.

John continued on at work but was very distracted, only coming home to eat and sleep occasionally. Behrooz was a ranting lunatic, which, coupled with all the whispering behind my back at work, was catastrophic to me and my mental health. Then came the day the police arrived at work to inform Emma her partner had committed suicide. I will never forget that day. Emma went straight to John, telling my son, "He's killed himself; you can move in tonight." The look on my son's face was disastrous.

Emma went off with the police to identify her partner's body. I went home to inform Behrooz.

We then entered a period of mayhem, Behrooz doing his usual woe-is-me ranting and raving, John trying to hold himself together, me going to work facing all the snide remarks, the silences when I walked into a room, the whispers. It was pure unadulterated mental torture; I did not think anything could get any worse.

Until a few weeks later when a gun-wielding gang robbed the store to obtain the Securicor cases containing twenty thousand pounds per case. My son and Mable were both on the shop floor filling up shelves when a regular customer ran in through the front door shouting, "You're being robbed at the back door!" Both Mable and John ran towards the back door, John getting there in front of Mable, tackling the robber who was armed with a gun. John could have been shot, snatching back the case from the robber, who saw the rest of the staff approaching and thank God, took to his heels, and left, with John passing the case to the store manager.

The police arrived, took statements – all the usual stuff. We all arrived home that night utterly exhausted to a ranting asshole whom I told to fuck the hell off, which gobsmacked him into one of his silences that lasted four weeks. But this time I couldn't have cared less; I was so traumatised by all these events.

By the end of those four weeks, John had moved in with Emma full-time. The funeral of her partner had come and gone, and her partner's mother and father, Grace and Malcolm, were now aware of Emma's affair with John and that John was living with Emma.

Time went on, shock after shock landing on all of us, as the police arrested John after the store manager accused him of organising the armed robbery. John was suspended from work while investigations took place. During these investigations, Emma informed John she was pregnant with his child; the shocks just kept coming. At home, we lived backing onto a massive green space that housed a sports club where events of all kinds took place regularly. One such event was a football tournament that descended into a riot, hordes of hooligans invading our houses trying to get away from thugs, resulting in our house suffering not just an invasion but substantial damage, along with the lady next door's house, which I obviously had to sort out, as per usual. Behrooz was incapable of doing so. On that day, I arrived home to confront a policeman who was supposed to be arresting the assailants sitting on my sofa, poo-pooing Behrooz. I told the policeman, "Get your arse off my sofa and arrest them for affray, assault with a weapon, trespass, and criminal damage." He was very startled by me, leaving our home to, as he said, try and catch some of them. Unbeknownst to me, this policeman had actually given one of the culprits a lift in his damn police car, as the next-door neighbour, Dill, told me when we discussed it all after it had calmed down a bit.

After I found that bit of information out, I was straight onto the police complaints, which resulted in a woman inspector arriving at our house, telling us she knew who the policeman who had attended our house was and admitting it was not the first time a complaint had been made against him.

I told her we wanted compensation to repair the damages to our property. She left, saying she would have to speak to her superiors. When she eventually returned to our house with paperwork saying that if we signed this paperwork, she could then get us some compensation, I told Behrooz not to sign that paperwork until he had the compensation in his hands. His usual answer was "Shut your fucking mouth, I'm signing this paperwork," which he did. The inspector said, "You will hear from us." As she left, I told Behrooz, "You did the wrong thing there; you will never hear from them again. By signing that paperwork, you have cleared them of any liability." Guess what? We never heard another word from the police, nor did we ever have any compensation from them.

I did, however, get compensation from the football club's insurance company after I contacted our local MP for help. The insurance representative arrived at our house full of himself. Before he came in, I rounded on Behrooz, who by this time was not only not speaking to me, but we had degenerated to my moving into our daughter's old bedroom, where I slept with a lock on the inside of the door and a wedge under the door at night, so if the lock broke,

I was still safe. We were living separate lives in the same house – fine by me, if still stressful.

I told Behrooz not to say a word to this insurance man and let me handle it. The insurance man was all, "Well, you know the club's insurance does not cover this type of incident." My reply was, "Okay, so let's put it this way: If you were my insurance company and we had a break-in at home, when you come out to assess, the first thing you would say to me is, 'Where is the five-lever lock on your door?' If we did not have one, you would deny our claim. So where are the football field's safety fences along the back of the houses to stop not only home invasions but footballs and all other projectiles landing in our homes? Pay up or see us in court. That's going to be great advertising for your company in the newspaper. We have the Coventry Evening Telegraph coming out tomorrow to do an interview." We got our compensation and an interview in the Telegraph, allowing us to repair all damages to our property.

It was as soon as one shocking situation seemed resolved that another reared its head or even overlapped. I did not have time to catch a breath.

When Tesco had John arrested, saying he was the organiser behind the armed robbery which had taken place a few weeks before, the police apparently had also arrested another couple of lads, one of whom had gone to school with John and whom John telephoned rarely for a chat. These lads were taken to various police stations around the city to be questioned. John came back to our house after midnight the next day, saying he had been released on bail as the police had all had to rush out to a local murder, so they could not continue the questioning. At that point, none of us knew the lad who had been murdered was someone both of my kids had been to school with, who was in the wrong place at the wrong time.

John had asked me that day what he should do about work. My reply was to go to work; he had done nothing wrong. Tesco had allowed John to arrive at work, let him fill his section, and put all the back stock away, then took him into the office and suspended him, never even asking him if he was innocent. The absolute filth of a company, especially considering he had risked his life tackling a gun-toting robber to get that case full of money back after that robbery.

It took two years from John's arrest to the time Crown Prosecution Service completed their investigation and cleared John of all wrongdoing. During that time, the union had come in telling Tesco they would have to reinstate John as a person is innocent until proven guilty.

At that point, I did not know the store manager knew full well who had actually done that robbery. Read my first book; it has all the details.

Too late for John by then, as he developed PTSD, which years later resulted in John being sectioned and never working again.

During those following two years, Emma got pregnant with my first grandchild, Jasmin, who, at the age of five months, ended up living with me full-time on a court residence order, as her mother had, like she had done with her older daughter, given her away. These children got in the way of her tarting about the city. By this time, John and Emma were splitting up and getting back together week after week.

John would phone me, asking to be picked up. I would go to him, finding him having to climb out of a bedroom window to get away from Emma, who would have locked him in the house, sitting with her back to the front door to stop him from leaving. A real nut job is Emma. John, by now, was realising exactly what he had gotten into with Emma; as soon as John had moved in with Emma, she had started tarting about with John's best friend.

After John came back home, he and his dad were not getting along at home, so John ended up getting a bedsit in Willenhall. Due to his mental health deteriorating over all the Tesco robbery stuff and Emma giving him the runaround, he had given up his job at the local Tesco and moved to a bigger store nearer to his bedsit. He was not doing well.

I had cut my hours back to half at Jubilee Store to enable me to care for Jasmin better. Behrooz was furious about me cutting my hours, as he wanted me to continue working full-time, basically to keep him and to continue as I had done all our married life, paying all household expenses. His philosophy was that I was to pay all the bills while his money went towards our retirement.

I never saw a penny of that money.

At first, when Jasmin had come to live with us, Behrooz seemed to have a change of personality; he was well into looking after Jasmin even though Behrooz and I were living separate lives. Then he started to pick on the child for the silliest reasons. I would berate him, saying, "That's a child; you are supposed to be the adult." What Behrooz did was throw away any chance he had been given to be a real dad the second time around.

It got to the stage where I dared not leave Jasmin on her own with Behrooz. He was not physically violent to her, but mentally it was really bad. John would walk from Willenhall every Sunday to be with his child at our home. When he arrived, Behrooz would make John stay out in the garden, no matter the weather, with Jasmin, where there was a teepee-type tent they could both sit in. Thank God Jasmin was young enough to think it was a game. While they were out there, Behrooz would be standing on the back doorstep, calling his son a cunt and a bastard and all other manner of vile things. I would get in front of Behrooz, telling him he was a disgrace and to go in the house and leave his son to enjoy his time with his child. The one thing that would stop Behrooz was the neighbours thinking Behrooz was anything other than a wonderful man. I would tell Behrooz, "The neighbours are watching you and can hear what you're saying." That would stop him in his tracks.

That was the last time Behrooz ever got the chance to be vile to any of us. The very next day, I was at the local bank arranging a loan with the bank manageress, telling her what was going on. Luckily, she had suffered domestic abuse herself, so she could understand what I was going through. To this day, I thank that woman. She told me, "Right, I'm giving you a loan for five thousand pounds; we will put it through as a kitchen loan." That enabled me to rent a house, buy a little second-hand car, and hire a van to move my stuff from the marital house.

Mable was fully aware of my situation; she had been telling me for ages to get out of there, but obviously, Jasmin was my first concern. As soon as she knew I was going, she enlisted the help of her three sons, all ex-servicemen, who arrived at my marital home with the hire van.

Behrooz was sitting in his usual position on the sofa in the lounge, shouting abuse at people walking by. "He's a fucking Irish cunt, he's a fucking paki bastard." He knew none of these people or their origins, and he knew he was safe doing this vile ranting as all the windows and doors were shut, so even if these innocent people heard him, they would have no idea where it was all coming from. I had sent Jasmin out for the day with her half-sister and her sister's nan, Grace, who was fully aware of the situation and what I was doing.

Behrooz saw the van pull up, stretching his neck like a turkey to get a good view of the van, saying, "What the fuck is that van doing out there?" My reply to Behrooz, as I opened the front door to let these heroes in, was, "They're here for my stuff. I am leaving you. I am taking half of everything and Jasmin."

That was the first time I had ever seen Behrooz speechless.

As the heroes started removing my belongings, taking only what I needed, as my solicitor had told me I was entitled to half of everything, I took the fridge, leaving the freezer and that sort of thing.

For all his big-man, I'm-God, you-will-do-as-I-say stance in life, Behrooz never said a word to my heroes, who totally ignored him.

As we left, Behrooz said to me, "Chris, why did you not talk to me about this?" My reply was, "Behrooz, I have been trying to talk to you for the last twenty-eight years. All I ever got when I did was physical and mental violence and abuse when I tried. The constant calling me an ugly, fat fucking cunting bastard, sick bitch – see a psychiatrist – when even trying to have a normal conversation with you was appalling.

"During those years, the only time you slipped up and showed the world your true nature and how you treated me was when you retired, and we had arranged with your one and only friend to have a bit of a do at your works clubhouse. As I walked in with the cake I had made for your retirement, you saw me and flew across the club, calling me a fucking sick bitch for not telling you about the party. All your ex-co-workers were shocked and appalled at your behaviour, saying to you, "Bloody hell, Behrooz, you can't speak to your wife like that, it's disgusting."

Even then, in your rage, you carried on and showed the whole world what type of man you really are. Did you not wonder why, within a few minutes of that scene, all your co-workers made excuses and left the club?

"I have been telling you since we first got married that if you did not realise just how abusive and violent you are to me, that one day you would be left on your own. I think that giving you twenty-eight years to try and alter the way you are with your family, even after a psychiatrist tried to tell you that you were wrong in how you have dealt with your family, has had no effect; all my begging and pleading has fallen on deaf ears."

I turned and walked away from the man whom I had loved, from the home I had built, but as I got into my car, a sense of peace came over me such as I had not known in twenty-eight years.

Mable stayed with me in my rented home for two days, which was situated at the other end of the terrace from her actual home, chosen for the fact I knew if Behrooz found me he would bring trouble to my door, and that my heroes were only a few doors away in Mable's house.

CHAPTER 15

After everything calmed down somewhat, I put in process divorce proceedings. At that point, Behrooz took out a case against me, telling all concerned I was a danger to my children and Jasmin and that I had been locked up in a mental institution, all totally untrue.

John was now living with me and his child, just how it should have been from the start. In fact, we all lived together until Jasmin turned nineteen and left home. John still lives with me as we are buying this house together.

At Tesco, I carried on working even though my mind was still in turmoil. At that point, John had been totally cleared of any wrongdoing around the robbery. Emma had moved on to bloke number three from John and was now in the process of actually getting married to bloke number three, who was a really nasty piece of work. She was also pregnant with his child, which turned out to be a boy. She now had three living children with three different dads, professing to have had miscarriages with bloke one and two after John. I personally believe there were no miscarriages, just false pregnancy stories to the men involved to try and retain them, but they were obviously made of sterner stuff than bloke three and told her child or no child, we are out of here. Bloke three was a muppet and fell for the baby story. Luckily for Emma, she actually managed to get pregnant, showing about three to four months after the wedding.

That marriage lasted six years before bloke three left her for another woman.

During this period of time, Jasmin had started to self-harm. Tesco would do nothing to help me as far as flexi hours were concerned, as I really had to be at home when Jasmin was at home.

When the case Behrooz took out against me came to court, the judge told Behrooz in no uncertain terms what a disgrace of a man he was, telling him, "You do not qualify for child residence; it's only biological parents who get that or a person who will be looking after the child full time – in this case, your wife." Behrooz actually stood up in court at that point to try and argue with the judge, who told Behrooz's solicitor, "You better take your client outside and instruct him in the way the court works, or you will both be in contempt of court."

The judge then gave me full custody of Jasmin and a full residence order in my name solely.

Behrooz was livid; you could hear him from chambers calling his solicitor all the names under the sun. His solicitor sure earned his money that day.

Once the court case was over and Jasmin knew I had full custody, she refused to have anything more to do with her granddad, fine by me as it was always a worry when she went to his house. The only reason he insisted on seeing her was the upcoming divorce; he did not really want anything to do with any family member but knew if he could tell the courts he needed the house to see Jasmin, the courts would not make him sell the house. Keeping our marital home was a key point to him.

The divorce was ugly; once again Behrooz wove a web of lies about not only me but his son and daughter, telling solicitors again I had been locked up in a mental hospital, that his daughter, who had a high-profile managerial job with AXA, was an alcoholic prostitute, and his son was a practising heroin addict. The lies and filth spewed just kept coming and coming.

That was when I had my accident at work, giving me a brain haemorrhage and disabling me, putting me off work for over a year. During this time, I really did not fully grasp what was going on around the divorce. To say my solicitor was great at the child case concerning Jasmin was fair, but they were absolutely rubbish regarding the divorce. It got to a point where my solicitor told me to just let Behrooz have the house as, at this point, he had kept me tied up in litigation for some six years. Her words to me were, "There will be no house left for either of you to have; it will all be gone in court costs."

Being not fully able to think right due to my brain injury and considering the fact that you have a solicitor you are paying to do the best for you and supposedly advise you correctly, I agreed to let Behrooz have the house. So, all the years of toil, saving shares, and money I had put into that house, which I had told my solicitor about, which she did not even check out, as she told me it did not matter. Yet my compensation from my accident at work was taken into consideration; they were even trying to sell my car from under me but couldn't as it was on hire purchase, which meant I had literally nothing from my twenty-eight-year marriage.

Yet nothing Behrooz was asked to prove, which was not a lot, was taken into consideration. What happened to all the money he was supposed to save for our retirement? Where did that go?

He would have seen us all on the streets with nothing: his wife, his children, his grandchild. The law in the United Kingdom stinks; it is very male-oriented.

But at least now I was free – no more terror for me or his children and grandchildren. To be fair, his son said to me, "Mum, I don't know if I should still keep in contact with my dad." My reply was, "John, he's your dad. I cannot make that choice for you; it's up to you." John has not spoken to or seen his dad since the divorce. Aslin is adamant she will never speak to her dad ever again. A few years after we split up, when she came back to Coventry from Yorkshire, she moved back in with her dad for a spell. I told her she could move in with me but would have to sleep on the sofa as all the bedrooms were taken. She said, "No, it's alright; I will move in with my dad and keep my head down." She was thirty. Behrooz gave her a curfew at the age of thirty.

One weekend, Aslin told Behrooz she was staying at her childhood friend's, which she did, returning on the Monday to find the front door locked. She rang the bell, and Behrooz opened the door, dragging her inside, kicking, and beating her, calling her a slag, then throwing her out onto the pavement.

Aslin called me in distress, and I quickly picked her up, taking her straight to the police station to file a complaint. The police arrested Behrooz, but ultimately, no charges were brought against him. Aslin stayed with me for a while until she found a flat of her own. At that point, we had to arrange to pick up her belongings from Behrooz's attic.

When we arrived, we found that he had padlocked every door in the house except for Aslin's room, clearly indicating his mentality. We had no intention of entering any rooms we didn't need to; we were not that naïve. None of us spoke to him or his only friend, who was obviously there as backup. All of Aslin's boxes were in the hallway, so we took them and left. We were in the house for no more than twenty minutes.

It wasn't until we opened her boxes later that we discovered he had smashed every single breakable item inside. I was furious and urged Aslin to go to the police, but she refused. For her, that day marked the death of her father. Even years later when she had her daughter, she never told Behrooz about Arden, Aslin's child. Jasmin, John's daughter, informed Behrooz about Arden, his second grandchild, but he never bothered to try to see her – the despicable man.

At work, Mable had begun a relationship with one of the men she was seeing. Previously, she had been in a six-month relationship with a man, even moving into his house, where he showered her with gifts and holidays. I never asked her why they split up, but I suspected it might have had something to do with a local alcoholic. His wife had thrown him out, and he showed up at Mable's doorstep asking to stay for a few days. Mable agreed, thinking it was a charitable act, but later revealed she was strapped for cash and had charged him three hundred pounds for the privilege. While he was there, she ended up sleeping with him, saying, "Any port in a storm." Oh my God!

With her current partner, Mable began spending weekends at his house while living in a flat during the week. Their relationship progressed to the point where she planned to give up her flat and move in with him full-time. One day at work, she excitedly told me they had bought a caravan to spend weekends by the sea. She invited me to help her clean and sort it out, and I readily agreed.

When we arrived at the caravan, we set to work cleaning. I scrubbed the filthy patio area while Mable cleaned inside. That night, as we sat down for a meal and a few drinks, Mable began sharing stories about her life with her deceased husband, Cedric. I think she underestimated my level of intoxication, as she spilled the beans about all her extramarital affairs while still married to Cedric. It was shocking to hear how she had been involved with the local bobby who was killed in the line of duty. Mable and Cedric had attended the funeral together, and she recounted how she had to hold back her tears, fearing Cedric would discover her true feelings. She confessed that if the policeman had lived, he was the one she wanted to spend the rest of her life with.

Talk about a female lothario! Poor Cedric had loved Mable passionately, completely unaware that he was married to a female Casanova – or maybe he did know. Mable also mentioned adopting Cedric's daughter from his previous marriage, but the girl wanted nothing to do with her. Perhaps the daughter could see through Mable's facade; who knows?

Looking back, this was when Mable started to pull away from our friendship. After that week of cleaning, she seemed to realise she had revealed too much. To be fair, I never divulged anything she told me until now, as I don't believe her grown children know everything about her. For years, I continued to try to maintain our friendship, but it became clear I was the only one trying to arrange outings. Eventually, I decided to wait for Mable to reach out to me first, but she never did. Our interactions became increasingly spaced out, and I found myself always making the first move until the friendship eventually fizzled out.

The final straw came when we had our usual monthly lunch with another ex-co-worker, June. Mable and June had never gotten along while we worked together, so I was surprised to find they had become fast friends. On this particular day, Mable informed me that Pat would be joining us. Pat had been one of my staff members while I was a manager at Tesco.

When Pat arrived, we had a great time chatting over lunch, and we arranged to meet again the following month. I offered Pat a lift home while Mable took June home, as neither of them drove. These monthly meetings continued for a while, with Pat and me joking about how Mable and June seemed joined at the hip despite their past antagonism.

Just before our last meeting, I received a text from Mable that was clearly not meant for me. It was a conversation between Mable and June, in which they spoke nastily about Pat. Shocked, I called Mable to ask if the text had been intended for me. She admitted it was meant for June, but I could tell she was caught off guard. She explained that she had only invited Pat as a one-off and hadn't wanted her to continue attending. When I asked why, she replied, "Well, she's not in our class," referring to her and June's perceived social status. Who the hell did she think she was?

If Mable and June were talking about Pat like that behind her back – and mine – what were they saying about me? I wasn't nasty; I simply told Mable I couldn't make that month's meeting, and that marked the end of our friendship. In hindsight, I realised that every time we had been together, the conversation had always revolved around Mable and what she wanted, with little room for anything else.

As time went on, my home life began to settle down. Jasmin was now under CAMHS for her mental health and received diagnoses of autism and ADHD. John was diagnosed with PTSD and schizophrenia. The landlord of our rented house was neglecting repairs; we had mould and mushrooms growing out of the walls. I was desperate to move and eventually secured a council house after being on the waiting list for eight years. What a blessing it was! Moving allowed us to put the past behind us and start fresh in a dry, mould-free home, which John and I are now buying.

Jasmin passed all her exams with A and A* results – not only because she has an IQ of 162 but also thanks to the tutors I hired to help her. After everything settled with her granddad, I managed to take Jasmin on two holidays a year through the Sun newspaper's holiday scheme, despite only being able to work part-time. Sometimes, I took her half-sister or some of her schoolmates along. We visited many fun parks, aided by the same voucher scheme.

Jasmin did not have a bad childhood in that respect. It would have been better if both her parents had been around like many other children, but all in all, she had a nan who loved and provided for her. Behrooz, from what Jasmin tells me, is still alone. She talks to him from time to time, usually when she needs money, which he readily gives, considering he was never there for his own children.

To this day, I cannot get over the fact that this staunch Muslim, who was so racist and derogatory toward all nations and despised all religions except his own, has now converted to Christianity. According to Jasmin, he wears a cross and has Bible quotes plastered all over the walls of his house. His conversion happened at his only friend's funeral, where he met an Asian Christian family who invited him to their church. When Jasmin told me about this, I replied, "I'm surprised he didn't spontaneously combust when he walked into church."

However, since that first church visit, he had to move to another church, telling Jasmin that the people in the first one were all really nasty. Knowing

Behrooz, I suspect he showed his true colours and was ostracised. Jasmin occasionally updates me on Behrooz, mentioning that he hasn't taxed or MOT'd his car for the last two years. He claims that God is watching over him and that he has stopped taking his medications because God has healed him; his spondylosis is cured because God saved him, and so on. I'm relieved she no longer visits him, as I believe all these statements reflect the ravings of a lunatic.

Aslin is doing well, now taking a university course despite her diagnosis of rapid cycling bipolar disorder. Arden has just started secondary school, and I hope she is okay after all the bullying she suffered at Moseley Primary School, which the headmistress, Niki Evens, failed to address.

In between leaving Tesco and being forced into retirement, I have now retired and enjoy writing books. I spend most weekends at local craft fairs promoting my work, even though my health is not great. You know, it wasn't until I met the Tesco pay claim solicitors in 2018 that I considered writing. While chatting about my twenty-six-year career at Tesco, one of the solicitors said, "My God, you should write a book." I replied that I had often thought about it, and that conversation led to my debut book, Sex, Drugs, Bread Rolls, and Armed Robberies, being published a few years later.

At that point, I had thought my life was quite humdrum, but writing my debut book proved to be incredibly cathartic. It allowed me to confront and put to rest some of the demons from my past. More than any therapy, it helped me realise that I am not worthless, despite what I had been told throughout my life. I had suffered abuse at the hands of my mother and subsequently my husbands, but through this process, I came to understand a powerful truth: no matter what any abuser tells you, we women are the stronger sex. We can achieve our goals, even if it takes us longer than we would like.

In my life I had the chance to be a Pub Landlady which got vetoed because Behrooz said I would be chatting up the men – my reply, yes, I possibly will be and their wives, it's called customer relations and how you build trade.

A golden opportunity lost because of a narcissist man.

A landlady, when we could have bought a new build house to rent out, lost because a narcissist said renters may damage the property; my reply that's what insurance is for, but not having enough funds back in the day to do it on my own, another golden opportunity lost.

My advice to any woman is you are worthy, do your own thing; no man owns you. If you have an idea that can make you money, do it, be self-sufficient. These days women have much better opportunities than we had in the seventies and eighties.

Be strong, beautiful, wise, wealthy and happy. In your own right.